Quantity Time

Quantity Time:

Words of Comfort for Imperfect Parents

by Roy MacGregor

M&S

Canadian Cataloguing in Publication Data

MacGregor, Roy, 1948–
    Quantity time

ISBN 0-7710-5442-4

1. Parenting   2. Parent and child.   I. Title.

HQ755.8.M24 1990   649'.1   C90–095012–9

McClelland & Stewart Inc.
The Canadian Publishers
481 University Avenue
Toronto, Ontario
M5G 2E9

Printed and bound in Canada

Contents

Introduction 7

Power Parenting 17

A Cry for Help 30

Just Kids 44

Wishful Thinking 64

Brain Surgery 76

Win or Lose 87

School Days 103

Lost and Found 114

The Dog 122

Holidays 132

Roots 147

Acknowledgments 157

Dedication

For Kerry, Christine, Jocelyn, and Gordon.

Introduction

This is all the result of an accident. None of it was ever supposed to happen. Five years ago, when the *Ottawa Citizen* hired me as a columnist, the editors simply handed over the real estate and said I could build what I wished on it. It seemed a dream come true. I thought – and believed they thought, as well – that the daily column we were discussing would be mostly politics. This was Ottawa, after all, and Parliament Hill had been my beat for the previous seven years. But they stressed that it shouldn't *always* be politics, and encouraging mention was made of a long-ago beat covering sports. Fine by me: Brian Mulroney on Tuesday, Wayne Gretzky on Wednesday. The column was launched and I went temporarily insane, as happens to self-important reporters lucky enough to land such work. Soon they would be recognizing me in the streets. My thoughts on the constitution would matter. . . . It took about a month before I realized that so many thoughts were available on the constitution that one extra simply vanished into the black hole readers were already skipping. And it took at least a year for a stranger to walk up and want to talk about a column – not the constitution, either, but what to make of finding a condom in the basement toy box.

Daily columnists, like shallow creeks, have a tendency to run dry. For weeks, there are more topics than chances to run with them: a cabinet minister resigns, a celebrity you once actually saw in an airport line-up dies, the twentieth anniversary of *Abbey Road* cries out for comment – and then, suddenly, there is nothing. You have no topic. There is nothing, absolutely nothing in the entire world worth writing about, not even the constitution. At dawn they fire.

It was during one of these mindless panics that the accident happened. During such crises, I tend to pounce upon a telephone before the first ring can pass; I jumped, and regretted doing so instantly. This was no tip that the government was about to fall, no collect call from George Bell. Just an old childhood friend calling to catch up. Knees twitching, palms sweating, heart pounding, I heard her out, more out of politeness than any hope for a column. After all, she was no elected official, no celebrity. All she was was the mother of three young boys. A funny, self-deprecating woman with the Irish gift of story, yes, but nothing to command invaluable space in a serious newspaper. Until, that is, she happened to wonder aloud if other parents, myself included, were as sick and screwed up about raising their kids as her.

She said she had been driving her grade-four son and his friend to school that morning and had taken the opportunity to remind them that they would be getting their projects back. The kids started giggling. "What's so funny?" she asked. "I bet you wonder if you got a better mark than my Dad," her son's friend said. "Don't be ridiculous," she told them. But she knew he was right; she did wonder. And not only did she wonder, but when her son returned at noon with a "B" she was furious. For days she and her husband – three university degrees between them – had stayed up past midnight, their son tucked into his flannelette sheets while they tucked into the *Encyclopedia Britannica* and various reference books on Egyptology. For a grade *four* project.

I knew from my own experience that she was not alone. But I had no idea how deeply this parental madness had set in until I called around and came up with a woman architect who had arranged the loan of a university laser for her daughter's grade-five science project, a city planner who had had to rent a truck to deliver his son's display, and a librarian who had caught parents tearing pages out of acid-rain reference books so no one but their very own junior scientists could win the ribbon. My friend was wrong: there were people out there even more screwed up and far sicker.

Desperate, and with no other topic calling, I wrote up her story, hoping that, at best, it would slip through unnoticed. No editor called, the column went to press, and what happened after that was the absolutely unexpected. The phone rang more often, people wanted to talk about it, the mail slot filled with letters, many of them confessional, and grateful teachers wrote with their own horror stories, some swearing that the innocent school project had gotten so out of control that from now on they would forbid their students from working on them at home.

As time went on, and as the well periodically went dry, I went back to children again and again. God knows there was no shortage of material. My own paper ran a fitness column in which parents had been advised to rub down their new baby's arms and legs with a toothbrush each day so that, a few years down the road, this early conditioning would pay off in an elite athlete. I heard about a university in California where fathers were taught how to shout through the abdominal wall of their pregnant mate so that their child would enter the world with a built-in vocabulary. It was as if the entire world had suddenly gone mad and no one had noticed: a respected university in New York was offering a course explaining "play" to parents who stood behind one-way mirrors watching their children fiddle with water; a day-care centre in Edmonton was offering computer training; a franchise had opened up in Montreal to teach busy parents how to enjoy "quality time" (in any other language, an hour a day) with their children; a woman in the United States was explaining why she had her secretary book her five-year-old's play time.

It was a gold mine beyond a columnist's wildest imaginings. While you might wait through an entire Question Period for a single lead, stories on what I came to think of as "Power Parenting" (a twist on politics' silly "Power Lunching") could be found anywhere and everywhere. A trip to the neighbourhood library turned up the full-colour, illustrated, *Tim Learns About Mutual Funds*. A man at work confessed that he had had to dip into his toddler's bank account to borrow for his own RRSP contribution. A magazine appeared on the news-stands with a feature article on how to take your toddler out to your favourite fancy restaurant: " . . . ask that beverages be served in small, flat-bottomed glasses, not stemware."

Eventually, the anecdotes begged a question: how did today's parents turn into creatures who *wear* their children rather than *bear* them? Perhaps it was inevitable. These parents – among whom I am a charter member – are the post-war Baby Boomers. Everything they had ever been interested in, the world had been expected to be fascinated by as well. If commitment was the main focus in the sixties and self-centredness in the seventies, then, of course, babies had to be the number-one world agenda item for the eighties and nineties. The world had survived the rebellious years; the world would have to survive the child-bearing years. These people would, in their own minds, be the first human beings in history to produce offspring, which naturally followed suit from being the first human beings in history to discover sex. Davy Crockett caps had been the rage; the Beatles had been the rage; Japanese imports had been the rage; houses, careers, minivans, and, above all, children would be the rage – and they are destined to remain so until such time as these strange creatures move out of their fertile years and the focus of the world can be shifted on to a new rage, be it condominium golf course developments, menopause, or bypass surgery.

But there is more to it than just the demographic control of fads. This generation – thanks to the invention of the Pill – had managed to become the first to put off becoming parents until the vast majority of them were absolutely ready for such a dramatic change. Once it became possible to control birth, the act of giving birth became more like the act of buying a house. Both could be put off until the time and finances were right.

Having a child then became an *investment*, just as buying a house always has been. Children, more than ever before, became possessions, possessions that (again like the house purchase) cried out for peer approval, and – far more importantly – possessions that led parents to look for a good return on their investment. A generation earlier, parents had wanted the best *for* their children; in the 1990s, parents want the best *from* their children.

That's why today we have a trophy for mere attendance at T-ball. That's why a worthwhile play group must end with a framed certificate. That's why children have a tougher timetable after school than during. That's why you find a doctor in Toronto's fashionable Forest Hill district doing a mail-out to competitive coaches within a thirty-mile radius, a computerized form letter detailing the scoring abilities, playmaking talents, character assessment, sweater number, dates and exact hours of practice and games, arena addresses, and the personal telephone number of his eight-year-old hockey-playing son. This is just one story among millions in a genetic mystery: how are these parents who once marched for equality for all today producing only above-average, extremely gifted children who either are in enrichment classes or are somehow being screwed out of them by the system?

For the most part, these poor wretches cannot help themselves. They have had the luxury of both time and money to indulge themselves with their children just as they have been indulged throughout their entire lives. School-oriented, they come from a life of courses; from work management retreats to Tuesday night golf lessons in a high-school gymnasium. Life must have organization and measure. Somewhere there must be a payoff. In the world of fast-food fathering and mothering, a certificate proves they cared, proves they were there when it mattered.

A lot of what they do is hilarious. These are, after all, the first males in history who can do a pelvic tilt. They are the first males to believe that a $500 "Empathy Belly" – forty pounds of bulging gut, complete with falsies and a shoulder harness – will give an understanding of what it is to be pregnant and carry a child. In wanting to be far more involved, far more intensely, in their children's lives than their own parents were in theirs, they can often be forgiven for what amounts to nothing more than too much enthusiasm.

But much of what they do is not so funny. For six years we have lived a typical Canadian suburban existence near Ottawa, in a house backing onto a schoolyard in which there are three baseball diamonds, a basketball court, two soccer fields, and, in winter, a flooded rink. In those six years I have not seen a single scrub baseball game played, though the summer evenings ring with the voices of mothers and fathers urging their youngsters on toward the league trophies. When the parents' lawn chairs fold, the game is over and the diamond is never used again until the chairs are laid out again, until two fathers can fill in a scorecard, the adult coaches can give in their line-ups, and the paid adult umpire gives the signal to begin playing again. I have seen two pick-up hockey games, and, for the first one, I had to explain to the kids who gathered how the game can indeed be played without referees and a clock. I have seen the odd kid shoot baskets. I have never seen a chance soccer encounter – never.

These seasonal observations have forced me to conclude that if this overbearing generation of parents
leaves one mark behind before it passes it will be this:
they stole play from their own children. And it is not yet
clear whether play can ever be returned to its rightful
owners.

This has been the ultimate selfish act. A generation
that eulogizes its own childhood is turning out children
who will have but one shared memory of their earliest
years: the view from the back seat of the car as they were
chauffeured from one sign-up to the next. Some might
argue that they will not need to recall anything more, for
everything else will be duly recorded for posterity on
the family Camcorder: filmed, edited, and backed by a
suitable soundtrack of sixties' tunes.

Where did this distrust of idle time begin? The children are not out in the park playing because they have
lost their desire to play. They are not there because, to a
large extent, those few who are home and at loose ends
cannot find anyone else at home to play with. Everyone
has other commitments, just like their parents. If a
neighbourhood playmate *is* found, the lucky ones can
play together until the telephone rings with news of the
next carpool. If, on rare occasion, two happen to be
found, one will have to go home, because this generation of parents doesn't think their child can play with
more than one other child at a time.

And better they play where we can see them – inside.
The park, even in the backyard, which was so recently
the glory of the young imagination, has today become
the equivalent of the fifties poolroom. Time on your
hands means trouble brewing. An *un*busy life is seen as a
threat, a risk that cannot be taken, and the result is

parents who feel a desperate need to control every situation, every outcome. If they had given birth to bonsai trees, the world would be more beautiful for it, but they gave birth to human beings, and what has happened is not pretty at all.

I did not notice it happening, but before long my column had become – at least once a week – a crusade for letting kids be kids. Some might fight for a strong central government: I was fighting for play.

This argument could only be made through stories involving my own children and their friends, which is dangerous ground. Little children learn to read. Their friends read. They look for themselves, disappointed at times when they find themselves, disappointed at other times when they don't find themselves. There is no easy way to handle such responsibility. My own inclination has been to treat them and their friends as "generic" kids, unnamed children, belonging to everyone. Any columnist who has ever dealt with personal issues cringes at the thoughts once expressed by the *Chicago Tribune*'s Bob Greene: "I think I have lost the ability to live my life if it's not going to end up on paper," and it must be said here that there is much more to any life than will be found here or placed on paper by any hand. Nor is a family in print a family in perfection. The people who follow aren't even close, but they are fortunate to have remained a family when so many others have not. And fortunate, too, to have been able to afford the lunacies of modern family life when far too many others cannot.

These columns – this book – came about by accident, but it is not an accident I regret. The experience has forced me to explore my own vast failings as a modern parent, forced me, as well, to speak out in defence of children with a passion I could never bring to, say, the constitution. And it has taught me, whether by accident or not, which of the two is the truly important issue of the day.

Power Parenting

May the gods have pity on today's parents, for no one else – most certainly not their own children – will forgive the current madness.

History may well record that at a certain point toward the end of the twentieth century, childhood was destroyed by those who should have known better. And for all we know now, history may pinpoint that ugly moment when childhood died as the month in which *Redbook* magazine allowed Dr. Benjamin Spock to advise parents to begin assigning chores to the two-year-old child. Presumably, for gifted children (and who today would dare not have a child destined for enrichment?), such work programs could begin the moment baby first learns to pick up an object. Better a dirty sock than a soother.

Historians may also turn to the narrow 4–3 vote cast by the members of the Los Angeles Board of Education, a vote which is almost certain to launch a trend to put schools on a twelve-month calendar. No more summers off.

And, finally, historians may puzzle over some wire copy that moved across Canadian Press that fateful week, a fitness column instructing today's parents to take a toothbrush to baby's legs and rub along the inside and outside of the tiny limb "to tone foot muscles and stimulate body awareness." A hair brush and you may well end up staring at a policeman's badge; a toothbrush and you're looking at an Olympic medal.

According to Janine Levy, the author of *Exercise for Your Baby*, baby fitness – from tummy massages to leg bounces – will enable the infant "to face the initial difficulties of life in the best condition." Once, in a distant and mist-shrouded past, this was foolishly referred to as "playing," but that, of course, was in the days before it became necessary for all that a child does to serve an ulterior purpose, a payoff. Those days are sometimes remembered as the pre-history of childhood, a time before everything that mattered could be measured by an appropriate certificate.

In the latter part of the twentieth century playing has been replaced by courses. And this has affected even those parents who hang onto their naïve notions of play the way others hold on to their belief that the world is flat, for their children have also been enrolled at the appropriate gymnasium, Y, ballpark, and community centre. If they were not, these children would go through life convinced that they were freaks of nature. Never seeing other children – because they were all either at their courses or *en route* to and from – these poor creatures would have to conclude that they were simply miniature adults.

It is precisely this Victorian notion of the child as miniature adult that has reared its head. Spock thinks they should be put to work; Los Angeles thinks they should regard school the way real adults deal with real work; Canadian Press thinks they should have a training program. Will parents soon cease speaking of potty-training and brag instead of personal bests? Will children, like domestics, require a law restricting the number of hours each week they can be on call for work around the house? Will June schoolyards soon cease to screech with the sweet melody of "No more teachers, no more books, no more teacher's dirty looks"?

But it is just no longer possible, says Dr. Charles Ballinger of the San Diego school system, to justify kids having the summer off. In his learned opinion, we've moved beyond "a nineteenth-century agricultural-economic schedule." The children will understand: *sorry, but no more nineteenth-century agricultural-economic schedule for you. This summer you go to school. And when you're not in school, here's a list of chores for you to do around the house. And when you're not in school and you're not at work, you should be working out, or, at the very least, taking this toothbrush to the inside of your little brother's legs so he'll have the same chance at life we've given you through such sacrifice.*

These are the parents, remember, who revolted against their own parents only twenty years ago. One can only hope that, before another twenty years passes, history will repeat itself.

It is only when you live within sight of a park that you come to realize that hardly anyone ever plays scrub these days. Rare is the day when you can listen in on the harmless banter of knocking-out-flies, a game of one-on-one over at the basketball court, touch football in the fall, or even pick-up hockey in the winter. These days, if you are interested in locating average kids at play, it is necessary first to look for the kitchen calendar of average parents. There, as strategically documented as a cabinet minister's daybook, it is possible to find out precisely when the fun has been scheduled.

"I don't know what we're going to do," a dedicated mother of three was saying at a recent five-pitch game. "This Wednesday we've got six events going on at the same time."

She certainly has our sympathy, for she speaks for a great many. This dilemma is all too common today, though such a situation would have been beyond belief thirty years ago. Back then, today's parents were yester-day's kids, and though it may seem hard to believe, back then they often resented being tied down to even one scheduled event a week, be it Cubs, Brownies, or church. But this, of course, was in the days before the child became the head of the family.

It may be that today's parents have spent so much time in the educational system that many of them have come to believe that life is an endless timetable of matters that are first measured by qualified instructors and then for-mally certified. Whatever, somewhere along the line, simple play became a difficult course. Like school, it had to be passed to be enjoyed. And, again like school, far too many parents began to have high – often unreason-able – expectations.

The sexual revolution, for all its good intentions, may have inadvertently had as large an effect on becoming a parent as it did on not becoming one. Once birth control turned having children into a conscious choice for most, roughly equal to buying a house, kids began to be regarded more and more as possessions. And once babies stopped looking like Winston Churchill and began more and more to resemble cars and stereos, they had to perform.

If, as they say, raising a child costs $150,000 today, then who can doubt that today's parents are looking to get their money's worth?

That is not the child up to bat, not the child vaulting, not the child raising the recorder toward its mouth: it is the Modern Parent, the parent who did not just *have* this child, but who designed and constructed and paid for it, and who is now being marked on the project.

There are moments when it's hard not to feel that if the kids had any control, they'd let Dad field the ball (which he really wished he could do anyway) or turn over the uneven bars to Mom. But kids, of course, have no control. They are the heads of the families only insofar as all decisions revolve around them, but they do not actually make them. They do not sign themselves up; they do not chart out the kitchen calendar; they do not drive.

It is during those drives to ball/swimming/gymnastics/ballet/hockey/Guides/skating/music that so much of this becomes apparent. The child whines in the back seat while the parent in the front whines about the incredible sacrifice in money and time. The gist of the adult argument is that, while the child may not realize it, all this is done so the kid can have opportunities the parent never had. Strangely enough, the back-seat tears are being shed for precisely the opportunities the parent did have –

the chance to do nothing, to call on the gang and see if anybody might like to go fly a kite or root around in the creek for crayfish.

Unfortunately, when you call on the gang these days, there's rarely anyone home.

This one we should have seen coming – *Dad, The Magazine for Today's Involved Father.* I found it on the local newstand, red-and-yellow lettering shouting "Premiere Issue! Premiere Issue! Premiere Issue!" across the top, a sloppy-looking, middle-aged guy on the cover with his eyes bugging and his hands over his ears.

There is no explanation why he's doing this. It can't be because he's just read the contents. If that were the case, his hands would be over his eyes, surely.

"Welcome to *Dad*," the editorial burbles, "the magazine for you, today's involved father."

The New Jersey publishers plan to put out six issues of *Dad* this year. And they obviously think they've just tapped into a ready market. "Until now," the editorial burbles on, "'parenting' was practically synonymous with 'motherhood.' Your significant roles as nurturer, protector, teacher, guide and special friend were neither addressed nor met on a regular basis. *Dad* was created especially to help fill this void."

Nice words, but what do you make of a magazine that claims it is dedicated to fatherhood and offers as its very first feature article, "Is Vasectomy For You?"

And what do you make of a magazine that preaches the joys of family life and offers as its very first colour ad a photograph of a two-seater sports car?

In fact, it is entirely possible to read the premiere issue of *Dad* as a rant against ever having kids.

- Page 6: How Much Do Kids Really Cost?
- Page 7: Is the High Cost of College Really Worth It?
- Page 10: A review of a hot new video, *See Dick & Jane Lie, Cheat, & Steal: Teaching Morality to Kids*, with an added editorial note that, "Since 1950, murder by teenagers has increased 232 per cent."
- Page 15: Prevent That Heart Attack.
- Page 20: A feature article on the "positive and constructive" side of "daydreaming."
- Page 21: A review of a bedtime story book – without illustrations – in which Merlin advises the little princess just to doze off and "perhaps you will *dream* a solution to the problem."
- Page 24: A coach's advice list for fathers, number two being: "COMPLAIN. Don't let the bad guys get away with it any longer that they should. If you know a system or program is detrimental to your (and everyone else's) kid, why just accept it? Your job, Dad, is to complain about it and see it change."

You begin to get the picture. If you haven't sent out for anti-depressants by the time you're two-thirds of the way through, you'd better quit while you're ahead, for the last third is entirely devoted to how awful life as a father can get: the difficulties in blending two different families togther in second and third marriages, the difficulties of life as a single father, the difficulties of life as a father whose children don't live in the same country, the agony of breaking up, how to deal with death, job change, relocation.

Dad does try to cheer you up a bit in a tail-end book review – " . . . all the basics as well as the latest informa-

tion available about AIDS, sexually-transmitted diseases
. . . Illustrated with warm, sensitive drawings," but by
then it's too late. Like the poor guy on the cover, you
can't take any more. Perhaps his eyes are bugging out in
such astonishment because he himself has just finished
Dad's feature on "The Toddling Gourmet," a step-by-
step manual on how to take children who still eat in high
chairs out to eat at "fine restaurants."

"When possible," *Dad* advises, "ask that beverages be
served in small, flat-bottomed glasses, not stemware."

This is not – repeat not – intended as satire.

But *Dad* does serve a useful purpose. It makes you
grateful, for once, that the kids are screaming and yelling
and fighting so much that you can't find five minutes to
just sit down and read a simple magazine.

A man I know – and it is worth thinking of him as a man
who brings his lunch each day in a brown paper bag –
was talking the other day about his child's birthday
party.

"I sat down when it was all over," he said, "and I
simply tallied up what I figured the presents he ended up
with were all worth. The total came to somewhere
around $400."

The Corporate Child of whom he spoke is three years
old.

"It's madness," he said. "Something's gone seriously
wrong with birthdays."

Evidence of this sweeping madness is all about us. A
seven-year-old tells her parents that she either has to
have a sleepover – which works out to twenty-four

hours of rented movies – or else she has to have a single party with a guest list of only nineteen. A parent rents an entire public swimming pool for their daughter and the chosen few. Another books her child's party for Sunday brunch in the dining hall of one of the city's most prestigious and expensive hotels. At the age of eight, they will be able to reminisce over brunch of birthdays once spent slumming in the McDonald's caboose. One may even have a story of a poor cousin who was forced to blow out the candles in the tacky setting of the family kitchen.

Do not be fooled into thinking that common sense rules on any street anywhere, not so long as balloons will float from front-door latches. Hardly a weekend passes anymore without a mad dash to K-Mart in hopes of solving the crisis for $10 – wrapping included. Yes, it is fortunate indeed that presents are, by custom, looked upon in the spirit given, not the spirit bought.

The birthday card is a simple matter, for it is essentially trade between grown-ups: selected by one, duly noted by another, completely ignored by both child and guests. But somewhere along the way, no one seems to know precisely where, it suddenly became vastly more expensive to hold birthdays than to go to them. The time when the hot dogs, Kool-aid, and Betty Crocker cake could be easily balanced by such gifts as forty-nine-cent, red-white-and-blue rubber balls, Pez dispensers, marbles, plastic purses, cheap doll dishes, and free samples from the Avon representative have long since passed.

"Where did these loot bags come from?" the man asks over his brown-bagged lunch. "I never even heard of them until we had a kid."

No one knows where the idea of the loot bag originated, though some anthropologists have argued a direct link can be made with Father's Day and stuffed baby chicks for Easter. What is known for certain is that the average Canadian loot bag contains $6.31 worth of stuff that has the capacity to rot the scoop off a city garbage truck. My own theory is that the loot bag was created as a desperate act of revenge by the first parent who ever said "Yes" to a sleepover. Since the parents or parent who had been lucky enough to dump their kid off the day before had just enjoyed twenty-four hours of human behaviour, the least they deserve in return is a kid guaranteed to bounce off the ceiling until midnight Thursday.

One wonders where all this is leading. If today's parent is booking brunch tables for children's birthdays when only a generation ago they themselves would have been content to find that their piece of cake contained a nickel wrapped in wax paper – what will the next generation do? Will today's children grow up and organize world cruises for their children's birthdays? Will they wrap BMW's in wax paper and coat them with cake and icing? Will they one day replace loot bags with sugar futures and investment certificates? Will tomorrow's parents wax nostalgic for simpler times, when McDonald's was enough?

The man at lunch has no idea where all this madness will go. He does know, however, that in his opinion, it has already gone too far for him.

"You know what's really bizarre?" he asks. "My kid's three years old and he's already got more money in the bank than I had when I got married."

His lunch finished, he carefully folds the brown bag to

use again tomorrow. Saving already, one presumes, for next year's birthday.

Soon it will be Sunday night: time once again to begin the failure tour of the house.

Last Sunday there was a judo belt tied to a banister. The nearest doorframe was cracked where some six-year-old Tarzan had used this vine to swing into the teeth of a crocodile. There was water-soluble children's make-up a foot deep in the bathroom, and old grown-up clothes from a green garbage storage bag strewn where they had been exchanged for a stunning summer-dress-torn-baseball-uniform combo. In the basement where there should be bare rafters and hard cement, there was a castle made out of old blankets, complete with work-out gym, dance floor, and bloodied battle-field. There had been angry phone calls all day long to settle a dispute between a seven-year-old Scottish-Irish Canadian and a five-year-old Japanese-Ukrainian Canadian as to which of them had more royal blood in their veins. And, of course, there was the usual detritus of a typical lost weekend: Dinky toys parked under chairs, flashlights taped to shoe boxes, dolls tied to handkerchief parachutes, bathtub filled with rubber ducks and plastic warriors and wooden spoons. . . .

Soon it will be time to walk around again and wonder where it all went wrong.

Each weekend begins the same way: I get up, I plan something worthwhile, educational, profitable, enlightening, invigorating, something brilliantly organized, conceived, planned out, and awaiting execution – and each weekend they give back the same response: *Bug off. We just want to play.*

There's something wrong with this picture, obviously. Here I am, offering them superior, enriched play – play with a purpose, play with a payoff – and here they are, weekend after weekend, telling me to bug off. Who has gotten to them?

Do they not know that in the Modern Age idle time is wasted time? Do they not know that today's perfect parent has learned to distrust time spent in a not entirely productive manner?

Bruno Bettelheim argues that the devaluation of play in the modern age is creating human beings who do not know how to deal with failure. "Play teaches the child without his being aware of it," says Bettelheim. "He learns not to give up at the first sign of failure, or at the fifth or tenth, and not to turn in dismay to something less difficult, but to try again and again . . .

"Perseverance is easily acquired around enjoyable activities such as chosen play. But if it has not become a habit through what is enjoyable, it is not likely to become one through an endeavor like school-work."

Can you believe it?

There's another guy named Weiniger who is going around arguing that "Playing is the way children learn what no one else can teach them."

And there's some Swiss psychologist named Piaget who says, "Every time we teach a child something, we keep him from inventing it himself."

The audacity, the nerve, the total blind ignorance.

I am even told that New York City's Columbia University has started up a course called "Discovery for 2's" which is intended to de-pressurize today's parents from meddling in their kid's play. The poor parent gets to watch the child do something goofy and useless like splash water while a professional psychologist holds the parent in a hammer lock and explains that the kid is all right on its own, that water can actually be splashed without Daddy or Mommy being there to guide the activity to some profitable, measurable conclusion.

Did you ever hear such lunacy?

It's blasphemy like this that is ruining my weekends. I bust my gut organizing something beneficial. I figure out the timetable, the seating arrangements, the amount of time necessary for travel, what they'll see, what they'll learn, and when they'll laugh. And what do I get for thanks?

Bug off. We just want to play.

A Cry for Help

I hate to do this to you, but I have to talk to someone about my sex life.

It's not that I'm completely mixed up about what comes before the cabbage leaf or the stork or before the cat heads out to drag something in out of the rain, but it still has to do with how we got here.

I once believed we came from dust and we return to dust, just like it says in the Bible. But nowhere in the Bible – and believe me, I have been looking – do I find the slightest reference to cute sperm and synchronized swimming. And that's why I have to talk to someone.

Sex used to be so simple anyone could understand it. It was taught in the street.

- You got pregnant from toilet seats.
- Only girls got pregnant.
- You used a word for a sex organ, you got slapped across the face.

Literature on the subject was kept on the highest rack,

right behind the hand-written sign that said "No Browsing!" What could be simpler?

But then along came this thing called "the Baby Boom," and an entire generation of lunatics got to pass through puberty at the same time as the Pill went through National Health and Welfare. They struck out on their own the moment some pervert in California invented free sex.

Soon they began ridiculing their own incredibly uptight parents over the silly way they had dealt with an absolutely normal thing like good, healthy sex – and they made solemn vows they would never be so foolish when the time came for them to deal with the simplest subject in the world. No hauling out the stories about storks and cabbages and cats. Just the bare facts, thank you.

How could it be otherwise, after the Pill, Woodstock, and 150 pre-natal classes? After all, this was the first generation in history where everybody not only knew precisely where babies came from, they knew four names – Latin included – for every part and function.

But then the day comes when you find the seven-year-old sitting at the kitchen table drawing pictures of absolutely enormous human appendages.

No . . . big arms and legs were last year.

And then the eight-year-old – who only last week was discovered in the school washroom turning herself and a friend into Tammy Faye Bakkers with their mothers' makeup – asks if you'd like to hear the new song that's going around the schoolyard.

> We are the pinkie girls,
> We wear our hair in curls.

We wear the shortest skirts.
We are the biggest flirts.
And when we kiss the boys,
We make the loudest noise.
We are the pinkie girls.

There's even a boys' verse:

We are the muscle boys.
We are the real McCoys.
We wear the tightest pants,
To give the girls a chance.
And when we kiss the girls,
We make them lose their curls.
We are the muscle boys.

Two verses of that and we were racing to the video store to rent *Where Did I Come From?* an animated film that is supposed to do the job you suddenly find you can't. We see the body parts. Fine. We see them in bed. Fine. The sheets begin to shake. Fine. But then we see one tiny little sperm swimming up a pink channel.

Soon there are hundreds of little sperm racing in a pool towards a frilly-dressed egg. And then they all break for a little synchronized swimming, complete with classical music.

"Cute," the eight-year-old says.

The movie ends, the sky darkens, another movie goes in and the children doze off.

The second film is a comedy. Real actors, not cartoon characters, end up shaking the sheets as well.

The seven-year-old stirs. "They're having sex," he explains carefully.

And on the movie rolls, the television glowing in one corner, the Modern Parent in the other, not wondering where he came from, but how he got here.

It is the nightmare shared by all parents of young children, hirers of babysitters, owners and renters of video cassette recorders.

You are hurrying out the door on a drizzly Monday morning to make the rental store before work, the tapes sliding in your arms like loose eggs, and suddenly you notice that the driveway is blocked by police cars. At the curb, Mounties wait on horseback. High over the birch, a helicopter churns, searchlights trained. The streets beyond are filled with worried priests, concerned ministers, fuming, finger-pointing evangelists. The lawn is fertilized with media, cameras waiting, microphones pointing out the guilty. And at the foot of the drive, the neighbourhood has gathered in force. They lean over the young and the innocent, shouting for answers to their incriminating questions.

"Where did you see the naked breasts?"

"Where did you learn the F-word?"

"Where did you get that joke about the twelve-inch penis?"

And one by one the small witnesses break, their chubby fingers rising to stab you to the heart.

"T-t-there . . ."

Someone calls for a rope.

The tapes fall from your arms, as they always do, and when you rise again the nightmare, unlike the cloud cover, has suddenly lifted, the police and priests and purple parents vanished into the mist. But you know it will come back, as it always does on Monday mornings.

It is this problem the tape rental outlets desperately need to address, not the current concern that sits on the front desks of most these days.

As you pay for your videos, you will discover a pile of pre-printed messages waiting on one side, messages you are invited to send on to the prime minister. All that is necessary is to sign your name to the small card and drop it in a mailbox to be counted among those who are fighting Bill C-54.

According to the message you will be sending, Bill C-54 – amendments to the criminal code concerning eroticism and pornography – amounts to censorship which is "the most repressive of its kind in the Western World." By signing the card, you are asking the prime minister "to withdraw Bill C-54 immediately."

I have no trouble with that, none at all. What people get their kicks out of is no one else's business, so long as no one else is harmed by it. Consider the card mailed.

The problem I speak of is far, far more troubling, and it concerns not glossy magazines but those tapes that are carted home on rare weekends when invitations, baby-sitters, and a few extra dollars happily combine.

This weekend the rental was *Clockwise*, described on the rental box as "hilarious . . . enjoyable . . . a pleasure throughout . . . zany comedy." Nowhere did it say this: "At the very moment you are stepping through the gathered neighbourhood children on the way to the laundry for a fresh shirt, the sexy woman in *Clockwise* will say to John Cleese, 'Why don't we take off all our clothes?'"

And that is a very mild example.

When they were left with *European Vacation*, the innocents were also left with five minutes of the teenaged son examining the breasts of a foreign playmate.

In *Splash*, the kids who could read were able to explain the subtitle crack about the twelve-inch penis to those who could not read.

We've been luckier with *Cocoon*, however. No one in the neighbourhood has yet figured out what the old man means when he says he's so excited about getting back to his wife that "a cat couldn't put a scratch in it."

So it goes. In the search for the light and funny, Richard Pryor always seems to fit the bill, but only through experience do you discover the Pryor is able to increase the average four-year-old's vocabulary by 300 per cent in less than 110 minutes.

Revenge of the Nerds is absolutely charming, but it is more than a bit rattling to come in on a massive gathering of four- to ten-year-olds mesmerized by the episode in which the beloved nerds drill into the co-ed showers and drop down a video camera.

No, we do not need Bill C-54, but we do need something – perhaps C-54(a): *An Act in which no parent can be held responsible, either criminally or morally, for what the babysitter or the neighbourhood children, regardless of age, see or hear* (or in the case of *Splash* read) *on a rented videocassette tape.*

There seems to be so little time in this world that lately I have taken to worrying about what to worry about. It boils down, really, to a question of time management.

ith deficits, the Canadian Football League, eastern
Europe, the constitution, black ice, and Senate reform all
being perfectly legitimate causes to fret over, it is vital for
the overly concerned among us to get our priorities
right.

Which brings us to C-CAVE.

I came across this strange group purely by accident
when several parents gathered recently in a suburban
school to discuss their children's favourite playmate,
television. C-CAVE – it stands for the Canadian Coali-
tion Against Violent Entertainment – came to put on a
slide show. If you find that you have some spare time to
twist in the wind, you might like to consider a few of
their points:

- The average Canadian kid spends 6.5 hours a day in
  front of "the cool fire" of television.
- Between 1960 and 1982 there was a 450-per cent
  increase in the number of murders, a 1,000-per cent
  increase in rape.
- *The A-Team* averaged forty-six acts of violence an
  hour, rather tame compared to an hour of *Bugs Bunny*
  and *The Roadrunner*, which manages fifty-seven.
- "Studies have shown" that there is a "link" between
  what children see on television and what is later
  reflected in society.

Okay now, move your coffee off to the side and go
sneak a peek at those little ticking time bombs in flannelette pyjamas as they form their semicircle around the
tube. Now doesn't your tax hike seem pretty insignifi-
cant in comparison?

The only way to deal with this crisis, says C-CAVE, is
for you, as parents, to "turn television watching into a
positive experience." They suggest you "watch televi-

sion with your children," that you discuss with them
"how people can distinguish between the good guys
and the bad guys."

One has to wonder where C-CAVE gets its kids.
Somehow they are able to tally 6.5 hours of viewing a
day for the "average" child, without it ever once dawn-
ing on them that today's child uses television the way
previous generations used radio – as background.

No one could argue that there is no disgustingly useless time spent in front of the tube, but some of the most
exquisite art has been created by kids who just happened
to hold their board of directors meeting in front of old
re-runs of *WKRP in Cincinnati*.

C-CAVE recommends the likes of *Mr. Rogers' Neighbourhood*, *Mr. Dressup*, and *Captain Kangaroo* reruns, the
kind of quality programming that, for whatever reasons,
seems only to be watched by kids who have failed to
gain control of the converter.

As for pointing out the good guys as opposed to the
bad guys, any television watcher above the age of two
who has difficulties with that one was a danger to society at birth.

No, too much television is assuredly not good for
you, but nor should we assume that just the right
amount is just right. When C-CAVE treats the medium
like vitamins – arguing that "seven hours a week is
considered an adequate amount for young children" –
one can only laugh. One can only weep, however, when
the organization strives so hard to make its connection
between senseless violence and senseless television. For
all we know, it may be because there is too much violence in society that there is too much reflected on television, not the reverse.

It is worth noting, surely, that those of us who grew up with *Sgt. Rock* and *Tales from the Crypt* and, yes, *Bugs Bunny* comic books did not all turn into serial killers.

All I remember my parents saying was that reading all the time would ruin my eyes. And they were right.

As for watching too much television, I'd like to think they'd just say it was a waste of time, the same as C-CAVE. Most of us have better things to worry about.

Looking back now, I am struck by how harmless it seemed when it first appeared at the front door. A few stray wires, a plug, a small box, a couple of strange handgrips with colourful but meaningless buttons.

"My parents say I can't live without this for three months," the teenager from down the street says. "I'm going to prove that I can."

It wasn't readily apparent then, as he stood there offering this short-term loan, that the difficulty in going *without* is nothing, nothing, compared to the impossibility of living *with* what he held in his arms.

Nintendo.

How a typical suburban family had avoided this electronic cocaine so far was a bit of a mystery. The house it was entering was plugged with the essence of modern living: VCR, computer, tape decks from Fisher-Price to assault ghetto blaster. But no Nintendo. Never Nintendo.

That's not to say we were ignorant of how far this curious box has penetrated people's lives. We knew it took in one out of every four dollars that were spent on toys in North America last year. And we knew a woman who recently admitted that her husband hadn't been out of his pajamas once between Christmas morning and New Year's Eve. The reason? Nintendo.

Sick. Very, very sick.

"Sure," I said. "We'll hang on to it for you. No problem."

Hah!

That was before I knew that the Modern Marketer is twice as brilliant as the Modern Parent. The Modern Parent, you will remember, is the enlightened person who walks around saying things like: "Oh no, we've never allowed our children to play with guns." The kind of person who likes nothing better than to sit in one room reading *Town and Country Homes* while the children sit in another hammering a button every time Minnie Mouse – that's right, *Minnie* Mouse – has a chance to shoot a cat.

The purpose of the typical Nintendo game is remarkably simple. It doesn't matter whether you are Minnie or Bugs Bunny or Michelangelo, the Teenage Mutant Ninja Turtle – your assignment is to kill, in whatever manner you can, absolutely everything that gets in your way. The Pink Panther shows up – squash his head with a cement block. Sylvester the Cat? Blow him away. Kill, destroy, maim, wipe out, move on.

For weeks the Modern Parents sit and read the latest *Parenting* while in the other room the death toll mounts.

Word gets out in the neighbourhood and children we have not seen for years begin knocking at the door at 7:15 A.M., willing to play a little Nintendo while they wait for someone to wake up. The children learn new ways of sharing. Basically, it is this: someone plays and then, after a short discussion involving screaming,

strangleholds, boots, teeth, and tears, someone plays the
next game. At eleven o'clock on a school night we discover a seven- and an eight-year-old sneaking down to
slip in a few more games before bedtime. Kids begin
shaking down hot air registers, desperate to scrape up
another $1.75 and another night's rent of computerized
murder from the local milk store.

By the end of three months, you begin to think, the
kid will come back for his game and find nothing but the
Modern Family sitting around a pile of burning tires in
the living room, the rent unpaid, the car repossessed, the
latest game humming and plinking and zapping in a
corner while a single, huge eye in each shrivelled head
searches desperately for the next Daffy Duck to blast
into oblivion.

But then, unexpectedly, there is a knock at the door.
The boy from down the street is there. He wants his
Nintendo back.

"I couldn't make it," he says a bit sheepishly.

"No problem," you say.

We wouldn't have made it either.

There is a remarkable difference to be found in western
Florida, on the Gulf side of the Canadian State of Mind.
Not the palm trees, though they do tower above those
that have been so strategically planted about Disney
World and Sea World and even the Orange County
Mall. Not the salt water. Not the high winds. Not the
endless shell shops. The difference lies in the lack of
hand-held video cameras.

If central Florida is a fair indicator of family trend lines, then the truly modern American and Canadian family has become an on-going, continuous, constant series for television. The only difference between the truly modern family series and, say, that of the Cosby family, is that the Cosby family shows up on 40 or 50 million other television sets and the truly modern family plays on only their own. Perhaps on two, if they can sucker the grandparents or patient friends into an evening of watching the kids stand impatiently in front of a main gate while Mom pans the entrance, or the kids leaving a ride while Dad zooms in on the exit.

These cameras are everywhere – VHS and BETA, personally owned and rented – and it is impossible to stand anywhere on the grounds of a major family attraction and not see a half dozen or more in action.

The truly modern family films their arrival, their standing in line, their lunches, rides, sights, rests. At Sea World a man filmed his wife synchronizing her watch. In Disney World another man knocked his wife silly while panning the monorail, then barely restrained his *cinéma verité* instincts long enough to hand her a Kleenex for her eye rather than capture the tears in a more permanent and artistic manner. When Mickey and Minnie and Goofy and Chip 'n' Dale and Pinocchio and the rest of the stars come out for a late-afternoon walkabout in front of the Magic Kingdom entrance, it is no longer a genteel session for hugs and autographs, it is now a scrum.

Mickey appears with his sweet smile and white-gloved wave and he is instantly engulfed by VCR-toting parents, each shuffling and pressing for position, checking the lighting, and assessing the angle. And then, while the spouse not working the camera pushes back other children along with the parents who are still stuck in the Print Age, the chosen child is booted forward so the magic moment can be captured for ever.

It is, as they say on Parliament Hill, an ugly situation.

Twenty minutes later, at the stroller checkout counter when the young families are leaving, not a single video camera is raised, not a button pushed. This may be because both hands are necessary to carry off the screaming, screeching stars of the family video, but there may be another reason.

This, after all, is what the baby boomers had to become once they became parents. Television – what the boomers' parents thought of as an escape from reality – somewhere along the line became reality itself for these people. And unless something – whether a war or a wedding – can be shown on television, it simply could not have happened, could not exist. If there is no footage of the child in full tantrum, then there was no tantrum. And their trip to Disney World can be enjoyed later as the best things of life always come to the modern family – on television.

Strange, is it not, that in this same state, less than two hundred miles away, there is not a single hand-held video camera to be seen? On the main street of this old island resort of Fort Myers Beach the main attraction is not a killer whale that does flips or a man in a mouse costume, but a rear-end collision that draws twenty spectators and twenty different opinions – but not a single camera.

And here, as afternoon fades, there is no autograph session to be scrummed, but a brief moment when the ripe orange of a sun slips down into the Gulf of Mexico.

It is a haunting sight, the sun dropping as if from a table, the high winds scooping up white sand and whipping it low and graceful as drifting snow. An old couple in windbreakers stand by the water, their hands raised to their eyes, not with cameras but simply to screen.

"You really have to be looking," said an old woman from Pennsylvania who comes to stand here each day for the sun drop. "Otherwise you will miss it." She stares out, hand shielding her eyes until the sky is suddenly ashen, then dark. And when she turns it is to smile at a young couple running with their camera, too late.

Just Kids

"*D*aaaadd?"

The call comes from the front door, where they stand knee deep in a swamp of muddy runners and neighbours' forgotten coats, where the fall leaves are piled higher on the tile than on the front lawn, and where they have just been ripped into for the usual morning crimes: lost mittens, missed homework, unnecessary kicks, and frittered time.

Slowly, "Daaa-aaaad?"

Sharply, "What?"

"Were you ever a kid?"

They giggle, as if it could not possibly be so. And little wonder, given that they are among the chosen children of the decade, small household *objets d'art* for whom absolute perfection has become but the lowest common denominator. For parents to expect so much, to demand nothing less than excellence from each child, they must themselves have come to Earth as full-grown and fully formed human masterpieces, unable to accept failure and bad behaviour and lack of commitment in their small charges because, of course, they have never encountered such flaws in their own lives.

It requires a moment for reflection.

On Monday, when I backed the six-year-old against the wall and threatened him with reform school for taking a hockey stick to the legs of a sister, it did not occur to me that I should admit to that day so many years ago when, finally, I had an older brother down near the slab pile and within reach of the axe, and how he still wears the scar of that moment on his elbow. No reform school was required, and today there's not even a single point levied against my driver's licence.

On Tuesday, when the six- and the seven-year-old demanded they be allowed to quit school, they were treated to the standard lecture on how the law will keep them there until they are sixteen. And even then they would be fools to quit, for school is not only necessary and good for them, it is the only proven path to the suburban bliss to which all sensible children should aspire. Not a word was said of the three days I once spent hiding from grade six in Mr. Gerhardt's blacksmith shop, sitting with his blessing behind a pile of scrap iron while the teacher thought I must be sick and parents believed all was well and fine.

Were you ever a kid?

Perhaps if full disclosure applied to parenting as well as politics, a question like this would never need to arise.

When the ten-year-old comes home with a note about missed homework it is treated like a subpoena. Nothing is said about my brother who, throughout a seven-year high-school career, refused to go to school on Tuesdays and yet today is a happy, successful parent

who undoubtedly keeps such stories from his own children.

When the most talkative of the girls has been moved
to four different seats since school began a month ago,
she hears only of the disappointment felt, nothing of the
thousands upon thousands of hours her father spent in
detention rooms under forced silence. And when one of
the girls packs a small suitcase for running away, she is
told only of the dangers that lurk out there, never of that
treasured day back in grade four when her father and his
best friend packed up enough Oreos and bananas for a
year, turned their bikes down toward the railway tracks
rather than the schoolyard and left to make their own
way in the world.

Somehow, we got back. And somehow – though I am
still at a loss to say exactly how or why – it all worked
out just fine. You mess up; you survive. At least that's the
way it used to be before Nothing Less Than Perfection
would do.

Slowly, "Were you?"

Sharply, "What?"

"Were you ever a kid?"

"Of course I was."

They are laughing – and they are still not out the door!

Sharper, "What's so funny about that?"

All together: "You were a *baby goat?*"

That's ridiculous. It's obvious I didn't turn into a goat
until much later in life.

There is something about the night that changes them.
And changes you, as well. Something about the night

and the way light falls in from the windows and other rooms and something, most certainly, about the way this gentle half-light falls over their faces and highlights their breathing. There are times when the moon is right and the day has gone wrong when you will linger at a doorway and do nothing but stare like a fool at the passage of time. Stare like a fool and wonder what memories they are carrying with them out of childhood.

What will they remember?

Their cheeks are still scarlet from the day just past. They are almost branded with what happened. This one, you tell yourself, they will remember forever. They will tell their own children of that January when first the snow fell and then the rain fell and then the winds turned and the cold came rushing back in to turn their world to glass.

The sun was shining when they awoke and they had to squint to look out. The road was ice. The yard pure ice. In the far schoolyard the skating rink now ran through three baseball diamonds, a basketball court, a tot lot, the soccer field, and on all the way to the main road, where emergency salt crews were trying to turn the surface back to pavement.

We have all seen this a few treasured times in our past. And what we remember are not the crushed fenders and poor footing, but the few magic hours you once skated over a lake or along a river that seemed to go on as far as the imagination can stretch.

We put on our skates and simply headed out the back door. We stumbled across another yard, along a short path and up onto a field that was already filled with people out to prove to their feet that their eyes were right: on a day like this, you could skate forever.

The field was packed with youngsters with sticks and a hockey puck and, for once, no parents in the stands, coaches on the bench, breakout patterns, whistles, shouts, and clocks – just a gang of kids laughing and yelling and chasing a game that has all but moved out of their reach. There was an old man with old tube skates, his hands folded peacefully behind his back as he glided from the soccer field to the school. There were mothers pulling babies on sleds, toddlers on bobskates, teenagers with cameras – the glass field sparkling in the winter sun with the flame of perfect memory.

They skated from the rink to the ball diamond. They skated around the bases. They skated over the basketball court, through the tot lot, over the soccer field, up the bank toward the road, and then back down again like surfers on a solid wave. They skated until their ski jackets lay in distant piles and the sweat under their toques had turned their hair to wet swirls. They skated and laughed and lay down flat on their backs and sucked on the ice as if it were so wonderful it had to be tasted inside as well as out.

And when they were tired of skating, they took out their bikes and slipped and slid and fell over the ice until they made it to the nearest Mac's Milk for a small treat before quitting the most wonderful day of their short lives.

It is night now. The moon and the far streetlights make the road and distant field look like they have been painted glossy black and then streaked with running yellow. They lie there, their cheeks still burning with the warmth of this perfect day. You stand, watching nothing, wishing for everything.

Two of them are sleeping in the same room. One stirs and then the other, both looking up and smiling at this over-protective animal that prowls in the doorway.

"Did you have a good day?" you ask, not being able to resist.

"Fan-tas-tic!" one of them says.

"What did you like best?" you ask, desperate to know what words they will use to remember the day when their world turned to ice.

"Going to Mac's." one says.

"Yeah, Mac's," the other agrees.

Such sweet memories.

It is dark, a cold, cracking evening in early January when the Christmas spirit has dwindled to a few twenty-five-watt strings along the far street.

I find her in my headlights as they sweep across the dark of the schoolyard, and she is running as fast as she can in the other direction, away. She is running with all the might that a seven-year-old body can muster, her small feet finding the snow turns to fresh cement as she scrambles – a daughter fleeing in terror from her own father.

Later, she will try and explain what it felt like, how the only sound she could hear was the machine gun of her own heart and how she looked for a lighted porch but could find nothing but the night turning ever darker. But first it is the father who must explain to her. She knows that an older sister was coming to meet her as she walked home from a friend's after a heavy day of Barbies, but she could not know that her father, coming along from work, would run into the older sister and decide to turn back and offer a warm ride. When those family headlights fell upon the child they were seeking – blinding her so she could make out neither the car nor its driver – they did not offer a ride but a threat that had been building for weeks.

In the month leading up to Christmas, in this area and in several other neighbourhoods across this sprawling city, a car had pulled up to a child walking alone and an overly friendly man had leant out offering money, candy, a ride. So far, there had been only the offers, followed by wisely bolting children, but the incidents had been written up in the papers, talked about in the classrooms, and, at one point, notices had even been sent home from the schools.

The seven-year-old and all of her Barbie-playing friends knew the surface details by heart. These are imaginations, remember, capable of spending an entire day turning a cat cage into a doll's bedroom. Not even Stephen King could speculate on what such minds might place behind the wheel of the red car that had been recently observed with suspicion.

"Will you walk me down? Will you come and get me? Please?" It had gotten to the point where she would insist someone stand at the front door as she travelled to the very next house.

How strange to stand there, watching, participating freely in such overblown fear. . . . You, who had ridiculed a woman who came to visit in the summer and spent what should have been a lazy afternoon standing on a picnic table sweeping a far tot lot with binoculars – a modern lifeguard making sure her children wouldn't drown in reality. How many times had you shaken your head in astonishment and gone into that well-worn speech about growing up where sweeping headlights and slowing cars meant the chance of a much-appreciated ride, where a certain old retired gentleman would stand on the same corner each Easter and hand out candy to every child who passed by, where the only thing children were ever told to beware of were strange dogs?

A couple of weeks ago it suddenly didn't seem like the appropriate thing to say when, in another neighbour-hood of this safe city, friends briefly lost their six-year-old boy. The mother of the friend he was visiting called to say he had left, but he did not arrive until – after an hour of eyes feeling as if they were encased in lemon – a policeman delivered him home, safe and sound. The boy had merely taken the wrong turn on the street.

For weeks this terror of the red car continues until, with no further suspicious sightings, the notes cease and the talk turns to other imaginings.

On a bright morning she asks, again, if I will stand by the door and watch her go all the way next door. I tell her, once again, that this is getting silly. She walks to the end of the drive, stops, turns and comes back, smiling sheepishly.

"You don't have to watch," she says.

"I know," I tell her. But I stay there anyway, pretend-ing to check the far clouds for snow, until I hear the sound of another door open and close.

It is 6:22 A.M., the light inadequate, the coffee still to perk, a shower yet to come.

Dawn on a workday, and you sleepwalk into the kitchen, flick on the light, stumble blindly onto a chair, and stare down into a bowl. A bowl that contains not porridge or Froot Loops, but a heavy brown tadpole that waves back as it kicks toward the bottom.

In the next room there is another bowl centred perfectly on the coffee table, but this bowl, fortunately, is covered. The cover, however, has a hundred tiny knife stabs in it. Inside the bowl there are a hundred thousand tiny, slithering, tent caterpillars.

By the sink there is a jar that flashes with the red bellies of leeches moving by. Yesterday there was a frog, and when a back was turned and suddenly there was no more frog, there were enough tears to fill the plastic pool where the frog had been given a perfectly good home of moss and rocks and enough potato bugs to keep it, one would have thought, content forever.

Welcome to the season of tiny creepy-crawly creatures.

It happens every year at this time. There are bugs once again around the porch light. There is digging in the garden. Pools at the side of the road are filled with frogs and tiny black pollywogs and newts and walking sticks and mosquito larvae and small children who should have taken their shoes off first. The schools, now counting down the days with an intensity that would shame NASA, have turned to endless field trips and pond studies to fill in the torturous time before the slithering, slinking, darting, wiggling, croaking, snapping, scratching, blood-sucking, tiny human creatures can be returned to whatever holding tanks their parents keep them in over the summer. And, of course, there is simply the child's endless enthusiasm for anything slimy that can upset those older and wiser.

Last week, it was a full-grown groundhog that the six-year-old found sleeping by the baseball diamond, picked up and carried halfway home before the deranged beast scrambled away and off into the lilac bushes. Then there was the garter snake from the bike path, a "perfectly good" snake with one small exception: it had been run over enough times that, had it been taken to school as planned, it would have made better wallpaper than shelf exhibit.

There is a massive caterpillar nest in the birch. Your plans are straightforward: either cut it out and trample the branch the moment it strikes the ground or else climb up, douse it with gasoline and throw a match. The seven-year-old has other plans: she could keep them in her room, and, when they get older and larger, train them to form a shimmering green necklace that would perfectly complement a certain summer dress. And then, of course, one day they would be butterflies – or is it moths? – and just think, if they were all trained to hang on and flap their tiny wings, then her dream to fly would finally come true.

There is nothing you can do about this phase but pass through it. Spiders must be carefully plucked in Kleenex and dropped, ever so gently, out the back door. House-flies must be chased towards open doors where others are coming in. Frogs will be kissed, salamanders worn on shoulders, June bugs found in pockets. All because this is the season of the tiny creatures.

But no matter how you beg them or plead with them or even offer to pay them, at no time will they agree to

take the earwigs from under the doormat off to school.
Nor will they show the slightest mercy to mosquitoes,
which is some hope anyway.

The Haunted House. One might have thought that in
the age of subdivisions and renovations, it had become a
childhood experience that would never again be experi-
enced.

I was late hearing about this one, not being part of
that remarkable network that includes recess and swinging tires and the backseats of minivans headed off for
courses no one but parents would ever sign up for, and
was let in on the secret more out of necessity than any
sense of sharing some hot childhood news. Where the
story began no one seems to know. But it did eventually
hit grade six, and a couple of grade six girls took along a
grade two boy to see it, and by the time the grade two
boy rounded up some of his pals to investigate they
knew they had no choice but to invite me along.

The reason had nothing to do with risking life and
limb to enter a Haunted House. That they would happily do on their own. But they did need an adult to get
them across the busy road.

"Will you take us to the Haunted House?" they
wanted to know.

"There's no such thing."

I said this, certain there could be no such thing *here* in
an Ottawa suburb where they put up historical plaques
on houses that don't have the family room on the main
floor. Had an *old* house ever existed, it would have long
since been visited by either a bulldozer or the architec-

ture firm of Jacuzzi & Skylight. Whatever these kids imagined might pass for a Haunted House, I had to see.

After all, as for everyone born before they invented bedroom communities and paint-stripping, the mere phrase "Haunted House" brought back a flood of memories: Vincent Price movies, eccentric old recluses, abandoned farmhouses where a ten-year-old could put up his feet and enjoy a nice quiet rum-dipped cigar. The Haunted House was usually where you saw your first sunbathing magazine and then spent the next half dozen years convinced that, the moment you became an adult, someone was going to come along and airbrush out all your weird parts.

"Let's go." And off the four of us went by bike, off down the street and across the busy road until, eventually, we came to a small industrial park and then a field.

"I see it!" the kid who had come earlier with his grade six sister called out.

Off through the field they set, frantically pushing their bikes through mud and burrs and dead flattened grass until they came to a stand of scruffy pine half concealing a rundown and blackened farmhouse. Whoever had lived here had clearly given up before bailing out. The shed, the yard, the house – even the outhouse was filled with garbage.

Someone had taken an axe to the walls, stones to the windows. A couch had been burned and tossed. A refrigerator smashed.

"*Fantastic!*" one of the grade twos said. "Can we go upstairs?"

"No!"

"Why?" Their question filled with ghosts and rotting bodies and blood-sucking bats.

"Because you might fall through the floor."

"Can we just go up and look?"

"No."

"Please..."

"Only look. Up quickly and down. And don't leave the top of the steps."

Up they scrambled, eyes popping, each with a hand on the other's T-shirt.

"Wow!" the first to arrive at the top of the stairs shouted. "Somebody's been here!" "They were *smoking!* And there's magazines – can we go closer?"

"NO!"

They froze.

"And get back down here right now!"

They scrambled back down, certain the adult had seen something slimy and blood-curdling that they had missed.

"W-w-what's wrong?"

"Nothing! We're going home!"

Off through the mud and burrs and dead flattened grass we went, over the busy road racing for home, the kids like explorers who had just discovered a great treasure. The adult looking like he had just seen a ghost.

The adult measure of the day can be taken – even now, going on midnight – with nothing more than a quick glance at the laundry sink. The cheap plastic cowboy boots stick out over the sides of the sink as if he has somehow fallen in head first. But below the inverted boots there is only a muddy pair of corduroys, completely soaked, a sopping wet shirt, completely soaked, a pair of underpants and a pair of socks, all completely soaked and draining. Only the child is missing.

He is upstairs, warm and dry, wrung out and strung out on the last of the Easter chocolate and put to bed, finally, with his brief child's measure of the day – Great!

What the adult has seen of the day calls up other words.

There was the morning search for Band-Aids, the fight with the friend next door, the cat scratch, the fight to the death with the youngest sister. There were two solid hours somewhere around lunch in which he established a new world's record for asking "What can I do?" And, of course, there was the catastrophe – but more of that later.

"You promised," he says, the Band-Aids all placed, the sisters wandered off to other battlefields, the cat outside, the friend run off. . . .

"Promised what?"

"We'd go for a bike ride."

Most nights for the past half year or so it has been the way he falls asleep. "As soon as spring comes," the parent mindlessly says, "we'll get out on our bikes, right?"

He thinks now that spring has finally come. The thermometer is above freezing for the first time since the Hundred Years' War. There are, for those who look closely, bare and ugly patches along the side of the driveways. The air is strong with dog.

"You promised."

And so, off we go, tires spinning in the slush, brakes laughing on ice. We are the first bikers of spring, two lunatics heading off down a street where old men in rubber boots still stand in their driveways with picks and shovels, men who take the same satisfaction from

clearing pavement that small children find in lifting old
scabs.

At the end of a distant street there is a bike path
heading off into nowhere. We are the first to break trail
through the seeping crystal. He falls several times. There
are, from time to time, clear breaks in the trail, places
where you can feel the early spring sun on your bald
spot and think about the delights to come. Those are still
a long way off.

He finds a curling indent in the snow that has been
caused by melting around a branch and wonders if it
could have been a snake we just missed. He looks for
minnows in the brown water running off the fields. He
slips on the ice, nearly loses a boot in the muck, bogs
down on a slight hill. There is a thin pyramid of mud and
water up his back, thrown there by the rear tire. His arms
grow tired pushing through the snow; he drops his bike
in a puddle; he can't move another inch. There is a
quarter mile to go.

And all this is before the catastrophe.

Back home and changed, he heads out to see what has
become of the schoolyard and thinks the ice that has
formed over the ditch is as strong as it was last time he
skidded over into the yard. He breaks through, the soak-
ing as thorough as if he had, fully clothed, rolled off a
dock.

He comes to the door, shaking like the last leaf on the
birch behind him, the water running loudly over the
floor, the only warmth to be found in his tears. Ten
minutes later, having run out of boots, he is back out
again in search of more puddles, more mud.

An adult, who counts a day gone bad on nothing
more than a cross look, heavy traffic, a stiff memo, an

unexpected bill, a minor delay, would take a day like this and shudder. Yet the child who managed to shudder through this day has but one word for it: Great!

If only we could know what it is that we lose along the way.

Sorry, kids, I hate to tell you this. But I have gone through the thirty-page press release twice. I have gone through the twenty-page strategy paper, the twenty-nine-page profile booklet, the seventeen-page policy paper . . . and found nothing.

The federal government's Labour Force Development Strategy contains not a single word for young children who want to quit school and get a job. That's a shame, because it's a severe national crisis as good as the rest. The kid gets yanked out of bed and slapped down, in tears, in front of a nourishing bowl of Count Chocula so he can be dressed, between spoonfuls, and hurried off to kindergarten.

"I hate school!" he whines.

"Why?"

"It's too long and too hard."

"You have to go to school. It's the law."

"But I want to quit!"

"What would you do if you quit?"

"I'd get a job."

It doesn't matter the age or the sex, it's always the same end result. The grade seven kid comes up against a French test and wants to quit. The grade five comes home with a reading assignment and wants to quit. The grade two has a lonely recess and wants to quit. The youngest doesn't even get out the front door and he's begging to quit – and find a job.

I keep in my desk a section of the want ads where two young women who are not yet teenagers sat one evening and went up and down the Help Wanted pages circling all the possibilities that are infinitely more rewarding than long division. There are twenty-four circles on the page I have kept. They have concluded they are qualified as clerks at Mac's Milk ("full-time midnights"), artificial nail technicians, tele-marketing operators, bulk food sales people, landscape labourers, bingo operators, cashiers, video store clerks, day care workers, Harvey's helpers, pizza deliverymen, and gas jockeys. The wages, where listed, run upwards of $7 an hour, which must look pretty good to someone faced with thirty hours of school for a miserly allowance that, more often than not, is forgotten entirely.

But there is one listing on the page that has been circled twice and underlined: "Go-Go waitresses. Possibility $1,000 weekly, salary and commission." I keep the page to remind myself that sometime within the next few years we are going to have to have that talk.

But in the meantime, it would have helped all parents if the Minister of Employment had only drawn a small loophole into this Labour Force Development Strategy. Say one tiny provision whereby the child labour laws might be waived for a day or two or even a week. All that would be required would be a note from a parent, and, if the kid can land something, he or she can quit school and join the work force. They would find, of course, that there's not a lot of call for people whose entire repertoire of skills include inspired mud renovations of front halls; redecorating with boots, jackets, skipping ropes, and baseball gloves; milk destruction; an ability to listen to two different tape decks at once; tattling; picking up stray cats; staying up later than is good for you; telephone obstruction; and car interior polishing with tropical fruit drinking boxes.

But surely, they could find something. Coal mines, cotton fields, sewing factories – whatever it takes to put an end to whining about how a job has got to be better than school.

Not just any job. Politics, of course, would have to be ruled out. A week of Question Period, cars and drivers who take you wherever you want, first-class airplane tickets, and the dessert counter at the parliamentary restaurant and nobody – I mean nobody – would ever look twice at recess again. Not only that, but the money's even better than nude table-top dancing at $1,000 a week. And the work's not nearly so difficult.

But anything else and never again would we have to put a boot to the back of the school bag just to get them out the door.

This is an examination of the effects of high altitude on memory. Perhaps you know already what I mean. The same effect is found, though to a much lesser degree, in fancy restaurants. You arrange to go out. You dress yourself in strange clothes. You hire a babysitter, even if you already own the babysitter. You clean out the car so it looks like adults belong in it, and you drive, slowly, deliberately, to a nice restaurant where you have booked reservations with an adult, where adults serve you, and where it is quiet enough to speak in the grown-up voice you had forgotten you have.

And what do you talk about? You talk about children. Not just any children, but children that do not exist in any form throughout the entire universe. Children who are finally working out just fine. Children who are a thousand times smarter than the teacher understands. Children who have Olympic potential if they would just apply themselves. Children who really love each other, deep down.

It must be the air in fancy restaurants.

Three hours later you're home, and the babysitter has been on the phone all night, the six-year-old is tied to a post in the basement, no one is even in their pajamas, and the neighbours have come over twice begging them to keep the noise down.

But I think it's worse on airplanes. It has occurred to me that when I fly anywhere, somewhere around the thirty-five-thousand-foot level, I go temporarily insane. It may be the air, it may be the calming effect flying toward a known destination has, it may be the in-flight meals – whatever it is, something happens.

Let's call it the Madness of the Frequent Flyer. Everything but the plane is disoriented. Hotel rooms baffle when one wakes up in the dark. Meals are uncertain. Cities endlessly confusing. But once on the plane . . .

The seat goes back, the muscles relax, the brain goes *pppfffft*. In a fancy restaurant you at least have your partner to talk to – and to blame when all the talk is about children that do not exist – but alone in a plane it is only you with your thoughts. Flying high over Lake Superior I stare out over the low clouds and it seems I can see them cleaning up the garage, straightening their bikes, putting away their toboggans, sweeping up the December Cheesies. Over the Rockies I can see them in school, all four of them with their arms snapping into the air with answers. Late at night, with only a few winking lights down there in the Quebec countryside, I can see my children all tucked in and asleep a full hour before the death threat, their homework done and stacked like firewood for a year at the front door.

Heading back into Ottawa at the end of two weeks away I am surprised they are not there to meet me at the airport, standing together holding hands in perfect harmony, their latest certificates of accomplishment hanging from their necks. But, of course, they are never there.

The taxi pulls up and cannot pull into the driveway for the abandoned bicycles and toboggans. The only girl who is home is on her way somewhere and says "Hi" as if I have just come from the bus stop. The boy hits me because there is no treat for him in my luggage. There is a message from a teacher in a sealed envelope hanging from the refrigerator.

But the dog is there, sixteen years old and stone deaf but she still knows I have not been around for a while and she wiggles like a snake at the sight of me.

"Good girl!" I say as I lean down to pat her. "Good, good dog!

"I thought about you constantly while I was away."

Wishful Thinking

There are times when the child's innocent view of world tensions – *Why don't countries just get together and work things out?* – makes perfect sense. Recently, for example, China admitted that its tough, one-child-per-family policy is a flop. Unless they install a half-billion cold showers immediately, the target for the year 2000 is going to be overshot by 120 million screaming babies.

The Chinese need to get together with the Swedes and work things out. In Sweden, the government has announced that parents will be given eighteen months of paid leave following the birth of a child. That's a year-and-a-half off – at 90 per cent pay – for both mother and father.

That's 548 days off in a row.

That's 3,836 diapers to be changed, some worse than others.

That's 548 interrupted nights, 311 dawns to greet, 67 trips to the emergency ward – 63 for earaches, 4 to get the plastic top of the Wet Ones surgically removed from your finger.

That's 272 snowsuits to twist on, 196 tins of Penaten Cream, 5,497 soothers to wash the cat hair off, 15 fold-up, swivel-wheeled umbrella strollers to put out with the morning garbage.

Eighteen months off sounds like a pretty sweet deal at first, but eighteen months is also a pretty long time. Somewhere there must be a secret Swedish government study that predicts such leave would be followed by a mad rush to get back to work. And it would have nothing, absolutely nothing, to do with picking up that lost 10 per cent of wages – which doesn't even cover parking anyway.

Having recently elected to spend just two months at home on leave rather than eighteen, I may be able to offer comfort to those who spent the first half of their lives wishing they looked like Swedes and are now burning with envy that they can't work like them. There are, you know, certain advantages to the office that only become apparent when you no longer have it.

After 548 days at home, you will eventually come to realize the cleaning staff won't be coming in at night to mop out the front hall.

There is no data centre to call and scream at when absolutely everything that can go wrong does go wrong.

There are no men walking around here with screw-drivers in the holster, daring an S-trap to spring a leak.

Lunch ends, not with the two of you tossing American Express cards and fighting over who will sneak it onto their expense accounts, but with dishes – and Kraft Dinner to blowtorch off the linoleum.

There is nothing heartwarming about gossip here. There is no pleasure to be had in a 32 in spelling or a double detention when it reflects directly on you. The only affairs to talk about are current, and even the constitution begins to lose a bit of its glitter after 548 straight days of "distinct society" versus "notwithstanding."

There is no bulletin board on which to tack up vicious, anonymous notes.

If the baby's disrupting everything, leaving a mess and affecting morale, sending a stiff memo won't have much effect. Nor will a petition.

If one of the older children gets on your nerves, you can't merely transfer them out of your department.

There are no golden handshakes to offer the old curmudgeon who runs the corner store.

If you want to get away for a holiday, there are no convention facilities for stay-at-home parents. And if the staff thinks it could benefit from a weekend retreat where they can just kick things around, there's only McDonald's.

Laundry doesn't work quite like reports, either. There's no putting it off until next week, when – finally – all the material you need is going to be in.

Worst of all, though, there is not a single one of those 548 days when you will be able to come in through the front door, drop a briefcase to catch everyone's attention, moan for a drink, and listen with a sly grin while someone else tells the rest of the house to leave you alone because you've had a terrible day and you're too tired to be bothered.

Make no mistake – 548 days of paid leave and ain't

nobody ever going to try it twice. Which, of course, is exactly why they should try it in China.

Now that it is over, I will dare to ask the question. Whatever happened to September?

Not where did it fly to or anything like that – quite frankly, I'm delighted it's out of here – but why is it that the month of September has never captured the poet's fancy? We all know, and endlessly repeat, T. S. Eliot's branding of poor April as cruel. Shakespeare told us to beware of March, Gordie Lightfoot of November. But what of September? To anyone with kids heading off to school and themselves heading back to work, March and November seem like South Seas islands in comparison.

September is not only crueler than April and more dangerous than either March or November, it should arrive with its own stress chart. Forget the impact of being fired or promoted or even dying, and consider for a moment what the trauma of a typical September can add up to before it's through:

• 200 points. You screwed up with the registrations. You missed the minor hockey cut-off by ten minutes and they slammed the phone down on your ear when you called to beg an extension. Judo is on at the same time as ballet. New, required, absolutely-no-exceptions equipment for gymnastics, dance, karate, swimming, music, and aerobics runs to $4,278.23 above and beyond registration fees – which were themselves paid for by post-dated cheques that turned to rubber the moment you handed them over.

- 150 points. You can drive back Tuesday and Thursday. The neighbour can drive there Tuesday and Thursday and Saturday. That leaves no one to bring them back Saturday – which is beginning to look like a terrific opportunity.

- 150 points. This week there were two frost warnings. You haven't even thinned the carrots yet.

- 175 points. The first three teacher-parent interviews went splendidly. But you relaxed too much in the fourth, telling the teacher that you couldn't for the life of you imagine what homework for grade fours is doing to advance civilization.

- 80 points. You just discovered that when the kids charged you $5 for cleaning the garage out in June, they tossed out the snow tires.

- 200 points. A note comes home in the judo-ballet-gymnastics-hockey-swimming bag informing you that they will boil your child alive if you don't agree to work 106 consecutive weekends in the tuck shop and spend every Saturday night for the rest of your life collecting bingo cards "to help out the club." Parents not desirous of helping out can, instead, make a one-time cash payment of $322,000.

- 125 points. Your eight-year-old has been caught smuggling make-up to school and emerging from the girls' washroom looking like Elvira.

- 100 points. Dates on the kitchen calendar can no longer be made out for all the paper clips, staples, and permanent marker scribbles. Subtract 50 points for each day in which a speck of white space remains.

- 200 points. In the fourth week after the beginning of school, the children are all finally in bed by 10:30 P.M.

- 175 points. Word comes that your children are being stoned in the schoolyard and shunned by their friends' parents for not having socially acceptable labels showing on their new clothes. Kids wearing old clothes and hand-me-downs are being attacked before they even reach the schoolyard.

- 800 points. Add 10 points – up to maximum of 800 – for every telephone call you race for in a single September evening that turns out not to be for you. If a call does happen to be for you, don't bother deducting points – just don't hang up.

As you can see, the calculation of the September Stress Factor is fairly simple. Any score over 100 makes you a danger to your children's health, if not your own. A score over 1,000 and you're probably already under heavy medication anyway, or should be, so there's not much more you can do about it.

The best news is that you can automatically deduct 500 points just for making it to October. And cheer up – another couple of weeks and you'll consider blowing hockey registration the healthiest lifestyle move you've ever made.

❄

Believe me, I do not go into this rant blind, but some-body has to speak out in defence of flawed parents and imperfect kids. You won't read about it anywhere else these days.

For two weeks now, I have been hounded by guilt over an essay that appeared in the Saturday paper. Bril-liantly written, it was one man's paean to the delights of reading good books to an appreciative child. The essay was a fond account of the simple pleasures to be found in discovering, hand in tiny hand, the jazz influences of Dr. Seuss and the abstract truths of Curious George. Above all, it was an evocative description of spending "quality time" with a child.

That essay might have eventually driven me mad had I not accidentally re-read the editor's introduction to the author and discovered that this perfect parent – the true hero of this essay, not the child – was the proud father of five-year-old Jamie. One kid. "Our child," as in "our BMW." Top-quality, Consumers' Report-approved, next-year's-model child.

But what of those of us who have by intent or, more often, accident, gone beyond the count of the single perfect child – in some cases two perfect children – and have gradually lost all control of their lives? There is no quality time for such parents. No time at all.

These are the people for whom coming home at the end of a long day means going straight back to work. In our own lost cause, I am met by a hall clogged with sixteen snowboots, sixteen snowsuit sections and – since they only come in odd numbers – fifteen soaked mittens. Eight kids: a friend for each child that belongs. Who can keep their names straight, let alone their library cards?

So let us now confess some hideous truths.

"Television," the New York essayist tells us, "is a convenient scapegoat." Well, that's fine for him to say, but in our house we believe television was invented by the same gods that gave the world soothers, closed bedroom doors, and dependable babysitters.

The essayist goes on to promote the idea of reading a different book each night. A lovely thought – if only it worked. The kids I have dealt with all seem to use books the way they use rancid old favourite blankets. Repetition and familiarity are what seem to attract them at least as much as the opportunity for enriching experience. All the library books in Ottawa do not seem capable of competing with two hideous little frayed books in our house, one called *The Story of Toby*, the other *Two Stories About Rickie*. Sour of humour, whimpering, and up past David Letterman's bedtime, it is not Dr. Seuss they call for, but these two insipid but comfortingly familiar stories.

The thirty-two pages of Toby have now been memorized, thanks to an estimated three hundred readings. For a couple of years now, it has been necessary only to turn the pages mechanically. The only thing that changes is the kid. And after a while, even the kid memorizes it, which means you can't cheat or change.

In the case of *Two Stories About Rickie*, this has proved particularly irksome, as I have grown to despise Jet the Crow – the star of the Rickie stories – to the point where I fantasize new endings for it. Exhausted, I am droning on and suddenly it is: "And once Rickie's Daddy had finished clubbing the stupid crow, all of the rest of them lived happily ever after." Usually, the child is asleep by then and wouldn't notice, but somehow, I doubt our essayist would approve.

Then again, having a perfect child, neither would he understand.

What follows are merely the typical New Year's Resolutions of your average Perfect Modern Family – in all likelihood, your neighbours on both sides and across the street. Read 'em and weep:

1. We, the children, promise to carefully remove our snowsuits each day, having wiped off our boots before entering, and then to hang up both jackets and pants and set each boot over the register to ensure it is dry in time for school tomorrow.

2. We will guard our mittens with our lives.

3. We shall not rest until each and every garment is attached to a hanger and the front door area has been lovingly scrubbed down by small children who sing quietly as they work.

4. We will immediately turn to our homework, which will be done silently in rooms barren of electrical appliances save a single lamp. There will be neither complaints launched nor errors made.

5. When done, we will cheerfully offer to go outside and play – together and nicely. Once there, we will find endless things to do, all of enormous delight.

6. We will walk ourselves to the single, weekly activity of our choice, and we shall look forward eagerly to each session, missing none.

7. We will watch only television that will improve ourselves, and only when said television is not being used for other purposes by a parent.

8. Having set the table, we shall sit down to eat, always together, and clapping with delight as the plates are delivered. Once each plate is scraped clean, we will race to see who can reach the sink first and begin the washing.

9. Evenings will be spent vacuuming and picking up clothes and putting together games and toys that came with more than one part.

10. At a single snap of a parent's fingers, we shall scurry off to bed, first carefully getting into our pajamas, then separating our clothes into those that may be laid out for wear again tomorrow and those that – following several days of hard wear – perhaps may qualify for laundry, which we will do ourselves, carefully separating the whites.

11. Teeth will be brushed – up and down, digging in under the gums – each morning and evening. Vitamins will be taken faithfully. When we have coughs, we will not only happily take the green medicine, but clean up the spot the spoon leaves beside the sink.

12. Bread and milk will be carefully rationed. Ties will be replaced on bags.

13. A "treat" will be defined as nothing more than having the good fortune to accompany one's parent to a Mac's Milk – for milk.

14. We will sit where assigned while in the car, saying nothing but looking contentedly out whatever window we wish.

15. We will, of course, be in enrichment classes at school, and we will leave entirely up to our parents when they wish to drop this little gem in the company of the less fortunate.

16. A "fight" will be defined as a small disagreement over, say, who gets to take the library books back, and will be conducted entirely by notes passed through a third person.

17. A "friend" will be defined as someone who dresses nicely, speaks only when spoken to, has no interest in other children's toy boxes, and does quite well in school, but not quite as well as us.

18. The following words and phrases will never cross our lips in the year to come: "sleepover," "prize from the cereal box," "Why not?" and "You don't own me."

19. We will sign legal affidavits indicating we will show no interest in driving until age twenty-five, no interest in drugs or booze ever, and no interest in members of the opposite sex until we are at least eighteen and after the young man or woman in question has agreed to submit a *curriculum vitae* to our parents.

20. Using the money daft grandparents send us, we will purchase from our parents the right to take out the garbage, shovel the driveway, and cut the lawn.

If it's of any comfort to you, the families across the street, to each side and down the street as far as the eye can see are not absolutely perfect. Common sense would argue that, sometime before the year is out, one of these resolutions is going to be broken. Probably.

Brain Surgery

*T*oday, class, we will be going on a field trip to the teenage brain.

Followers of "Doonesbury," the cartoon strip, may recall how they were once sucked into a tour of Ronald Reagan's mind and ended up being shown mostly empty space, but readers should have no such fears about signing up for this one. After all, if there were any empty space to be found here, the average teenager would long ago have stuffed it full of dirty socks and underwear and overdue library books.

A $5 cover charge will be collected on the way in.

We will be entering the teenage brain through the ear. Be sure to turn to the right or left and stop immediately. If you go straight ahead, you'll have a long wait for the bus. The scar tissue you notice along the walls is the work of vandals whose names – Van Halen, Guns 'n' Roses, Def Leppard, Rob Base, and D. J. E–Z Rock – are known to the authorities. That stain on the floor is from

New Kids on the Block, who were allowed in by mistake and quickly asked to leave.

Past the heavily corroded ear drums, you will come to a small mass of cells. This is the teenage memory. It believes the world as we know it began in 1980, when a huge meteorite collided with Earth and killed off all the Beatles. Inside this most curious room of the teenage brain, you will find vague black-and-white and sepia thoughts of Dad as a severely balding child with beer on his breath and of Mom as a homely child from a family so poor they had to share curling irons.

Next door is the teenage grip on reality. Visitors are advised to hang on to the railings. Pregnant women and those with high blood pressure and heart problems should skip this ride. Inside, brave viewers will view a constantly changing flow chart indicating who is going with whom, who likes whom, who wants to dump whom, what is out and what is in, and all the current hot labels in cottonwear. Again, you must hang on to the handrails while viewing this area. Dizziness, vertigo, and nausea are normal sensations for first-time visitors, so please don't panic.

And don't be put off by the constantly ringing telephone – it's not for you anyway.

From reality we pass quickly into knowledge. A cramped room, it contains lyrics, telephone numbers, video dialogue, dates of upcoming parties, and floorplans of the major area malls. Those school science projects stacked in the corner have nothing to do with this room. They were sent here in error and are being held temporarily until they can be shipped to the brain of the parent who actually did all the work.

Directly above knowledge is the motor cortex of the teenage brain. It controls voluntary movement. Nothing ever happens here.

That big, pulsating maw of cells in the centre is the teenage view of sex. This is the largest room in the brain and the only one that constantly throbs. Maybe it's better if you don't look. But if you do, you will note that this section of the male teenage brain is completely out of control. The quieter the surrounding environment gets, the worse it gets. For this reason, no visitors are admitted during history class or homework hours for fear of personal injury.

This area of the female teenage brain is rather more difficult to appreciate. Those unable to pick up whispers and obscure body language would be wasting their time.

Farther to the left, visitors will enter the frontal lobe, which contains the teenage personality and is slightly less stable than the governments of Italy, Greece, and Lebanon. Those two figures slugging it out in the far corner are who the teenager used to be and who the teenager is going to be. Who the teenager really is varies from day to day and is on an unpredictable shift schedule.

Moving toward the back, we come to the occipital lobe, which is said to control vision in the human brain. Perhaps it does. In the case of the teenage brain, however, that job falls to another organ – the hand-held channel selector.

Visitors will note that there remains one area of the teenage brain that will not be visited, the teenage taste centre. Since the arrival of the new 2 Live Crew album and the release of *Friday the Thirteenth, Part XXXIV*, it has been closed for renovations. In fact, it is always closed for renovations.

A $5 advance on the next cover charge will be collected on the way out.

The response has been so overwhelming to our recent tour of the teenage brain that we have been asked to arrange a similar excursion into the mind of the seven-year-old. Those signing up will be required to produce a medical certificate proving they have had their nerves cauterized within the last six months.

There will be no departures scheduled after nine o'clock in the evening, so the chances of being crushed in a tantrum or read to death are slim indeed. Even so, travellers are advised to wear hockey shin guards, ear plugs, and dark glasses in case something goes wrong.

Unlike the tour of the teenage brain, there is no charge for this trip unless, of course, we accidentally stumble across a stand of coin-operated machines filled with jellied hands that are capable of picking up only dog hair.

We will be entering, as before, through the ear. Visitors will instantly notice the difference in decor. Walls that in the teenager were battle-scarred with rap music are here dripping and oozing on one side with Sharon, Lois and Bram, and, on the other side, rippling suggestively with New Kids on the Block. Anthropologists who have studied the interior of the seven-year-old ear believe it to be a classic example of where one civilization ends and another begins – though there is some dispute over whether "civilization" is a proper term for the stage this ear will shortly be moving into.

Beyond the ear, of course, we come to the seven-year-old memory. It is not large and it is always wrong. For reasons scientists are still unable to explain, it is capable only of remembering with absolute and perfect clarity promises that were never made, words that were never spoken, and incidents that never happened. It cannot, on the other hand, recall how on earth it got home from school with only one winter boot on.

Just to the left, we come to a vast storage area known as the seven-year-old brain's supply of irritating questions. Visitors are encouraged to try their luck:

• Who invented God?
• How far do I have to count before we get there?
• Why not?

Anyone coming up with suitable answers is excused from the rest of the tour. No one ever has.

Next to the endless vat of hopeless questions we come to a special chamber that is found nowhere else on Earth, with the possible exception of the brain of the male praying mantis shortly after mating and immediately before being eaten alive by its lover. This bizarre part of the seven-year-old brain is known as the where-do-they-get-such-ideas chamber, and it is filled with ridiculous notions. It believes, for example, that there is no reason it cannot have a hamster, a horse, a guinea pig, a new puppy, a kitten, a lizard, a gerbil, a living dinosaur, and six new goldfish for Christmas. It believes it is blamed for everything when it did nothing. It believes a week consists of seven sleepovers. It believes that, when cartoons are on, loud and repeated yelling of the word "Wait!" can actually stop clocks from ticking.

The activity in this area contrasts sharply with what we come to next – the seven-year-old brain's area of common sense. At this stage of development, this consists of a single cell and shows no signs of activity.

That slightly larger clump of cells towards the top of the brain is the seven-year-old's total knowledge. Mostly it is made up of lists of who today's best friend is, whose guts are hated, who hates your guts, and who was really to blame for what happened yesterday at recess.

But the seven-year-old brain also knows one thing that soon vanishes, only to be recalled years later by exasperated parents who wish they could somehow return to those times. And that crucial knowledge is that if you simply collapse in a pile and are willing to cry long enough and hard enough, someone else will do it for you.

Adult visitors have been known to weep openly when visiting this historic site.

Get out the Kleenex. No, this is not a farewell tour, but it's close.

We will be leaving this morning on the journey of a lifetime. As promised to all those who complained that we were trespassing without permission in their young brains, today we will begin a forced march through the mind of the forty-one-year-old parent.

Dress warmly. There are drafts.

We will begin, as always, in the ear. And don't panic, the bearer carrying that machete is only here to clear the path. The damage, you will note, is considerable; sort of a Mexico City of collapsed cells. You can see where Jerry Lee Lewis carved his initials, where Elvis struck, even where Iron Butterfly once flew past. You will note the forty-one-year-old's inability to absorb a single word when the eyes are distracted by a newspaper, book or TV sports.

We now enter the brain's basement. The shelves are stacked with an astounding variety of matters – the Pythagorean theorem, the chemical formula for soap, the plot of Silas Marner, how a carburetor works, and Jay's Treaty – not a single one of which makes the slightest sense anymore to the forty-one-year-old brain. Step carefully – the clutter is accumulating at such an accelerating rate that shortly this brain is going to have to open up its own landfill site.

Immediately above, you will see the brain's extensive alarm system, which was not necessary in the other minds we toured. What this does is alert the brain first thing in the morning that it is no longer twenty-three and it is about to discover things in the mirror that were never there before – or, in the case of hair, were.

We come now to ambition which, unlike the basement, is rapidly shrinking in size. That shelf over there is filled with regret, regret that you never got around to saving Africa from drought, regret that here it is 1990 and you still haven't gotten around to straightening up the garage. That big black mass over there is the place where they pile the dead brain cells. Don't ask. If anyone comes across the summer of 1970, however, we've been looking for it for some time now.

Just beyond we come to motor skills, and they definitely could use a good mechanic, this being the time of life when you finally get your backhand down the same week you go in for arthroscopic surgery, you have a choice of two shadowy holes to putt toward, and you

start needing your mother back in the dressing room to
do up your skates.

The closet to your right is filled with the forty-one-
year-old brain's sense of fashion. Inside, you will find
such delights as galoshes with rusty buckles, ascots,
amulets, bellbottoms made out of the American flag,
rum-dipped cigars, ties as wide as planks, sideburns, and
red handkerchiefs that tie just above the left knee of
obscenely torn jeans.

We come now to the forty-one-year-old brain's sense
of wonder. It no longer worries about things like Santa
Claus and space aliens, but about when you're finally
going to start acting as adult as adults did back when
you were a kid. Wasn't twenty-one supposed to be when
you were grown up? Then they dropped it to eighteen.
When are they going to admit they blew it and raise the
age of majority to sixty-three?

You might want to take a Gravol pill, as we come next
to the parenting section of the forty-one-year-old brain.
You will note the room is divided in half. That tidy,
organized half to the left is what should be done according to the books. To the right is what is usually done: the
baffles are to cut down the screaming, the weapons,
fortunately, are under lock and key, the closet is stuffed
full of bizarre variations on, "You really disappoint me,
you know."

That area which in the teenage brain was as big as a
gymnasium – sex – is, in the forty-one-year-old mind –
none of your business.

In fact, what are you doing here anyway?

❋

It is March. The weather is so unpredictable we can't plan on anything outdoors. The bank account is so low we wouldn't dare plan on going south. But that needn't keep us from a short trip that involves a little warmth, fresh air, and nearly forgotten light. It is the perfect time, surely, to head out on our long overdue tour of the grandparent's mind.

We shall enter the aging brain as we entered the unsullied brain of the seven-year-old, the unused brain of the teenager, and the twisted brain of the forty-one-year-old parent – through the ear.

You will note immediately that this particular ear has developed an ability to hear only what it wants. Go ahead, try it. Offer some well-meaning financial advice you've been building up for months to pass on and just watch the reaction. Nothing. Now say something – no, whisper something – about how this government seems to be doing a crackerjack job of managing its affairs. Stand well back.

Beyond the ear we come to perception. The reason there are nurses scurrying about and tubes running up into drip bags is because this particular area of the grandparent's mind is in a constant state of shock. Much of this is directly related to waste management, which you may erroneously believe would be controlled by another portion of the body. It is not. The waste control that drives the grandparent to distraction is controlled, in fact, by other brains that are linked only genetically to the grandparent.

We are speaking, of course, of the next generation down and of such things as VCR's in master bedrooms, three cars, March Break in St. Lucia, two showers a day, order-in pizza, video games, compact disc systems, summer sports camps, double-shifting nannies, and a dozen full green garbage bags at the end of the driveway every Wednesday morning.

You'd be in shock, too, if you had worked and scrimped and saved from, say, 1935 to 1980 to build up a retirement nest egg and, yes, inheritance, that the average modern family could blow in less than forty-eight hours.

A few steps beyond perception, we come to the grandparent memory, which tour operators are currently seeking to have recognized as one of the great Wonders of the World. You will note, for example, that there is perfect clarity surrounding R. B. Bennett's Great Depression radio broadcasts, what clothes were worn on VE Day, the precise idle setting for a 1953 Pontiac carburetor, the price of Cow Brand baking soda in August 1948, and the third verse of "Casey at the Bat." You will also note, however, that a dark, obscuring haze surrounds such items as where the reading glasses were last put down.

We come next to motor control. Step carefully, for there's a huge gap between what the brain wants and what the body delivers. The brain is filled with motor cells that were developed during ten-mile walks to school, skating from dawn to dusk, cross-country skiing before it became a fashion industry, and using feet on a Saturday night because no one ever had a car. The body, unfortunately, likes to pretend none of this ever happened and that the past seventy years have been spent snapping like an elastic band every time it eases into a chair.

That vast cavern to the right is common sense. No visitors under the age of fifty-five will be admitted for the very good reason that nothing they would see there would make the slightest sense to them. It is this part of the grandparent's brain that shuts the mouth when the grandparent sees the idiotic manner in which the grand-children are being raised. And it is this part of the brain that says, and keeps saying, that one day the rest of the world will wake up and see that life is something to be lived, not filmed on hand-held video cameras and played back later on the family television when there's nothing better to watch.

There is no charge, incidentally, for entrance to this room, and visitors are invited to take whatever they need when they go.

Win or Lose

*P*lease bear with me while I catch my breath. I'm beat. My legs feel like rubber. My knees won't work. My back hurts. My shoulders ache. I'm dehydrated, clammy, throat sore, heart missing, stomach churning, washroom calling. Medical doctors with children will immediately recognize the symptoms: the Modern Parent at the end of a child's competition.

Doesn't matter whether it's a hockey tournament, a baseball game, a gymnastics competition, or a Tae Kwon Do exhibition – it's always the same. The Modern Parent is so drained there seems nothing left to do but throw up, cry, tuck yourself in for twenty-four hours, and hope you recover by the time the next red-circled Saturday comes around to pound you senseless all over again.

The kid, meanwhile, is off somewhere goofing around. If he or she thinks of you at all, it is merely to wonder why, at the end of each one of these torturous days, Mom or Dad finds it necessary to take them aside, hug them like they're about to announce that grandpa got hit by a bus, and then recite this month's version of: "It doesn't matter whether you win or lose, only . ..."

Funny, isn't it? These are the same people who will legislate Truth in Broadcasting and vote for Truth in Politics. But what would they say if there were Truth in Parenting?

"Don't you understand? My whole inner being, my standing in the community, my life, depended on you cashing in on that breakaway!"

I have just returned from a gymnastics competition. I have watched a mother lunge from her seat high in the stands when her daughter slipped momentarily on the balance beam. I have seen another mother so distraught she found more comfort in the washroom than in her family. I have seen a foolish man fold his sweaty hands in prayer as a young girl ran toward the vault. I admit it – I am that fool. And when that certain girl was not slipping on the beam or in mid-air on the uneven bars, I spent the time looking around at what has become of us, the generation who once said they would shape a life where co-operation mattered more than competition.

In the stands, where blood pressure is well into stroke territory, only one man does not seem affected by what is happening. He sits, smiling, staring into the viewfinder of a video camera, undoubtedly so caught up with meters and gadgets that he does not realize his own child could, with a small slip, destroy his social standing forever. Obviously, he does not understand what it takes to be a Modern Parent at a sports event.

The true Modern Parent knows it is silly to say that sport builds character. It reveals it, and more often the character of the parent than the kid. That is why you have to watch so closely, pray so hard.

If the Modern Parent could only figure out how to become invisible, he would gladly become his son's goon winger during the hockey games, her daughter's footing on the balance beam. The Modern Parent knows the unfairness of it all. For years you have kept them from pain and harm and even hurt feelings. You have done their rationalizing and their crying for them. But now, much too soon, they are out there on their own – *and it just isn't fair!*

Little wonder today's little athletes have become walking sports medicine clinics, with weekly bookings at the chiropractor and equipment bags stuffed with Entrophen anti-inflammatory pills. It's not for the kids, it's for the parents – an explanation for whatever goes wrong. Obviously, she'd still be on the balance beam and headed for a perfect "10" if we'd only come up with the $150 for that crucial knee brace.

The meet finally over, the Modern Parent is deciding whether to call it a night or call an ambulance. But first he must talk to the smiling, sweatless guy with the video camera.

"Have a look yourself," he says. "It's like you're watching TV. It doesn't seem real. "I don't even know what happened until I get home and plug it into the set. By then it's too late to do anything about what happens anyway. It's history. It's fantastic."

I must get one of those. Soon as we pay off the brace.

Like everyone else, I have an image of myself that is kept tucked away for comfort on difficult days, much as old men will fold a twenty-dollar bill several times and slide it into a secret slip in their wallet.

The particular image I harbour of myself is wrapped in a hot summer's day. The sun is high in a cloudless sky, the winds calm. The only sound, apart from the occasional squawk of a startled blue heron, is the slight sizzle a canoe and paddle make over a river as smooth as shellac. I am fishing in this fantasy, a light rod sitting loose on the ribs of the canoe, the line stretching far and flashing lazy in the soft light that falls behind. There is nothing on the hook, nothing in the mind, nowhere to go and nowhere you've been.

It is early Saturday morning and I am putting on the image. The trunk is filling up with rod and tackle box and paddles and life preserver and cooler and worms. The head wears a baseball cap from a construction company. The jaw needs a shave. The sunglasses speak of mystery.

"I'm coming!"

The sunglasses pull down, revealing a six-year-old with a life preserver and a paddle so short it is better suited for cheese than water.

The cooler is opened. Another sandwich is necessary. He wants to take a supply of Popsicles.

"I'm coming!"

She wants time to change her dress. No, maybe she'll keep her dress on. She wants to bring her friend. He wants to bring his friend. They fight over what friends can go and settle on both.

The cooler is repacked. The trunk won't go down for lifejackets. They want to bring yet another friend they can share.

But friends don't come equipped. Old rods must be made up with tied-on line and leaders and hooks. One friend has a rod but it hasn't been used since 1763. The line snaps when you roll it softly between your fingers.

"I'm coming!"

She is eleven and she wants to come. She always comes, she says. It's not fair to take the little ones and not take her.

The sunglasses are off now; they won't stay on for the rolling sweat.

Finally we are on the road, the car bubbling over with rods and cold pop and treats from Mac's and life preservers and friends. Thank God the oldest didn't insist on coming. Thank God the eleven-year-old didn't demand a friend or else . . .

"Can we stop and pick up my friend?"

We are in the middle of the country. But she knows the way to the farmhouse. At the farmhouse the friend has a friend over already and can't come anyway. An hour to play with the new kittens, visit the dogs, run out and look at the donkey, stare at the cows, and we are off again.

We head first to the high side of a large dam, where the wind whistles in off the water so hard the first attempted cast sends a hook into the forearm of the seven-year-old daughter.

Thank God it's not one of the friends.

We retreat from the wind to a sheltered dock that has flooded over. A snapping turtle follows the first worm back and sends barefoot kids scurrying for the hills. It begins to rain. When they are not playing with the worms, they are caught on bottom, caught on each other, tangled, tired, wet, bored.

One of the friends latches on to a channel catfish, easily three pounds, and it takes five minutes of screaming to land it. The only picture she will agree to must be taken with a telephoto lens, with the fish well in the foreground and the girl so far back the two will not agree to focus.

Eventually the worms are gone, the pants are soaked, the fights are settled, the rods so tangled Rubik himself could not begin to sort them out. It has been a Saturday of sacrifice, one that should, if there is justice, pay off in a Sunday alone with the image. Tomorrow, the canoe and the sunglassed Outdoorsman will write poetry with a paddle.

This is the thought that comforts, the thought that shatters as the last one is tucked in and turns with a final grab at the day.

"We're all going fishing again tomorrow, okay?"

It has snowed through the night. Not much, but enough. The outer sill is covered with a thin, packy snow the texture of rabbit's fur, and the morning sun is just beginning to make it glass around the edges.

I see them first from the upstairs window, two boys in colours enough for a rainbow, and they are headed down the street in a manner that some of us believed had been lost to the mists and snowswirls of time. One has two wide shovels over one shoulder, a hockey stick over the other, his skates fitted neatly through the blades over the stick. The other has the skates and a stick as well, but a hockey net over the other shoulder – a net of bent, rusted aluminum and torn, ragged netting, the recipient of several thousand Stanley Cup-winning overtime goals.

They are a memory from the past walking through a neighbourhood that did not even exist when such

scenes mysteriously vanished from the Canadian landscape. But they do not wear dull ski jackets from the
sixties nor duffle coats from the fifties nor big sweaters
knitted with number-1 needles from the forties: their
arms, waists, shoulders, chests, glove fingers, thumbs,
and tuques are the kaleidoscope of the eighties. They are
for real, and they are off to play a game of shinny.

Their tracks lead to the park, in behind the school
where men come most nights to shovel and scrape and
flood with fire hoses and wonder why kids today are so
different than they were when *they* were kids. On this
sunny day, with a packy carpet of snow over the ice, they
have come from all directions, a dozen youngsters, a
dozen sticks, two dozen skates, two nets, and enough
shovels.

For more than an hour they work. The big kids
ploughing together with the larger shovels, the younger
kids doing the fine work. It is tough going and soon
tuques are tossed to the side to show wet, uncombed,
curling hair. Rainbow-coloured winter jackets soon follow, revealing a few hockey sweaters of the eighties. A
new Pittsburgh Penguin. Two fading Edmonton Oilers.

The ice cleared, these youngsters who have spent their
lives dancing around pilons and stopping at the fifty-
minute mark, who have been driven to every practice
and game, who have shown up or else, these youngsters
are ready to play shinny.

"Will you referee?" they ask the adult who has come
with his youngest to skate in the bare patch off to the
side.

"A referee? What for?"

"To do the face-offs."

They are lined up perfectly, a centre and wingers, defencemen back. The adult shrugs and agrees, picks up the tennis ball and moves to centre ice.

"Do you have a watch?"

"Sorry. Why?"

"We want to know when the periods are over."

The ball is dropped, a shot taken – deftly caught in a baseball glove.

"Face-off!" the goalie's defenceman yells.

The adult picks up the ball and moves to centre.

"Not there!" the goalie shouts. "Here!"

He points to a spot where – if this were a rink instead of a schoolyard and someone was paying out $65 an hour instead of nothing – the face-off would certainly be held.

They score and they line up again. No one announces the game. No one wanders off to eat snow. It is all so businesslike.

The ball bounces high off a defender's knee and is clipped out of the air by the Penguin's blade.

"High sticking!" someone shouts. "That's two minutes."

But no one, of course, has a watch. The Penguin, they decide, will have to stand on a snowbank while the goalie closest to him counts out loud to a hundred.

They want a face-off.

"I quit," says the adult.

"No! We need a ref!"

"You're better off without one."

The adult removed, they begin, slowly, to ignore the rules. No more face-offs but half ice. No penalties. Someone wanders off to eat snow.

Two hours later – the fifty-minute custom shattered –
they are still there, their boots and shovels holding the
far net down in the wind that carries their shouts and
yells and cheers back across the schoolyard like a breath
of fresh air from another time.

It is when they begin to make sense that you know you
are in trouble.

I am thinking today about a certain young man I
know and the way he begins each and every day of his
life: "Is there school today?"

Usually there is, and after a bit of whining, he heads
off reluctantly. On days when there isn't, he cheers. He
says he wants to quit.

"But what will you do?"

"Play."

There was a time when your line of argument made
some sense. You know it by heart: There is more to life
than play; Play doesn't put bread on the table; You're
going to have to have something to fall back on; Don't
forget your education . . .

The question we are forced to ask ourselves, heading
into the 1990s, however, is: does any of this make sense
anymore?

Not much, it seems, if you happen to play professional
sports.

It used to be that education didn't matter all that much
so long as you were Bobby Orr or Gordie Howe or
Mickey Mantle or O. J. Simpson. Superstars had it
made. But have you noticed what happened in the winter of 1990?

- Pascual Perez, a deeply troubled, at-times-drug-addicted pitcher who just finished a losing season (9–13) signed with the New York Yankees for $5.7 million.
- Bryn Smith, a journeyman pitcher (10–11 in 1989) went to St. Louis for $6 million.
- Mookie Wilson, an outfielder who was not so long ago having a tough time hanging onto his job, signed for $1.5 million a season.
- Tony Pena, a catcher who drove in thirty-nine runs in 1989, signed with the Boston Red Sox for $6.4 million.
- And, of course, pitcher Mark Langston just became the richest baseball player in history, with a five-year, $16-million deal.

The *average* baseball salary this season was $512,804.

But baseball players are paupers compared to professional basketball players. In the National Basketball Association the average salary is well above $600,000.

This has gotten so out of control that a poor player by the name of Jon Koncak – with an average of less than five points a game – recently signed a five-year $13.2-million contract.

Even in hockey – professional sports' "poor cousin" without an American national television contract – the average salary is now $200,000. That's Canadian funds, the rest are American, which makes the average, run-of-the-mill journeyman baseball or basketball player even richer than you imagined.

But even $200,000 a year Canadian sounds pretty good to engineers and PhDs and probably even to the odd doctor.

Why, then, do we still say it's good to have an education to fall back on? Wouldn't it be better to say it's always nice to have a career in professional sports to fall back on? Besides, have you taken a good look lately at what's happened to the Three Rs we all used to worship?

Reading's losing out to television.

'Riting now requires that you push control F2–3 and a complete and accurate spellcheck of your gibberish will be done in an instant.

'Rithmatic now is done by solar-powered pocket calculators.

Better that a child work on a split-fingered fastball.

And what about this "something to fall back on when your playing days are over" talk? Have you not noticed? They no longer end! Baseball players go to Florida to play in the over-thirty-five leagues. Old hockey players get picked up by the Los Angeles Kings for $600,000 a season. And just to settle the argument once and for all, who can name the world's fastest growing, most successful professional sport?

You got it – the senior golf tour.

The kid's right. If he really wants to get ahead in this world, he'll drop out of school tomorrow and start aiming at one day being just an average player.

It is not precisely certain when the hero worshipping of George Bell began. The one who worships is five years old now, and probably does not even remember the gods who preceded George Bell. First there was Bert of Bert 'n' Ernie, then came a dreadful period of looking up

to the Smurfs and Ronald McDonald. But in time the
gods came to take on more human characteristics,
though never quite totally real.

Pee Wee Herman was the first. Then came the Karate
Kid, a particularly dangerous period of worship, for you
never knew when he would attack – or at what height.

And then along came George Bell.

Why? It's difficult to say. Partly because the name is so
agreeable to a young mouth. Partly because of George
Bell's television spot for McDonald's. Partly because of
an eighty-year-old grandfather who insists on wearing
his own Blue Jay's cap whenever the Toronto ball team
and George Bell are on his overheated television. Whatever, sometime last summer the then-four-year-old
began watching out for George Bell with a passion not
even Bert 'n' Ernie at their height could match.

It began when a small colour stamp of George Bell fell
out of a cereal box and showed up in the evening licked
and slapped onto the headboard of his bed.

It continued when the Blue Jays entered the stretch
drive as genuine contenders, and George Bell's familiar
batting stance appeared on the sports pages. The wor-
shipper would cut Bell out, head upstairs with the
Scotch tape, and a half hour later there would be a whole
roll of tape and a small, poorly cut picture of George on
the wall. When George Bell was voted Most Valuable
Player, he cut the picture from the front page and pasted
it up. He cut out and pasted when George Bell had his
big salary fight, when George Bell signed his multi-
million dollar contract, when George Bell took his time
coming to camp, when George Bell took offence at the
attempt to remove him from left field and turn him into a
designated hitter only.

By the time the five-year-old left Canada for Florida two weeks ago, his bedroom had become a shrine. He knew next to nothing about Bell's remarkable statistics and absolutely nothing about George Bell's remarkable temper. All he knew was that he was going to Florida and he had just cut out a full-colour picture of George Bell in Florida. How could they possibly *not* run into each other?

At Disney World he asked about George Bell, at Sea World, at Busch Gardens, at a hundred different McDonald's, on the beach, in the pool, every night before bed. Finally, on the last day, George Bell could not be put off any longer. As they say in baseball – there was no tomorrow.

On the drive up to Dunedin he pulled out a loaded water pistol and wanted to know if it was all right if he shot George Bell.

Probably not, he was told, unless there was still enough of the Karate Kid in him to fend off a drop kick to the throat delivered by a 194-pound DH wearing metal cleats.

It was a magnificent day for a five-year-old's very first baseball game – azure sky, warm again, the ice cream cheap – but somehow, the game meant little. If he had picked a best play, it would have been the three-wheel machine that dragged away the batting screen. But there was a brief moment during batting practice when – with his journalist parent safely out of drop-kick range – the hat he was wearing left his head and entered George Bell's hands, and a moment later was returned to his head with a quick "G. Bell" scribbled below the insignia.

The moment was precisely as the five-year-old had imagined it, a mortal of pure faith in easy touch with his god. It was why he had come.

Eventually, the game began, and when they sang "O Canada" he ended by locking his hands in prayer, but whether it was simply a reflex from kindergarten or something more complicated is difficult to say. All that is certain is that by the top of the second, he was dead asleep.

And not even George Bell's baseball bat could have knocked that hat out of his hands.

It is the great Unspoken Tragedy of modern life. There are grandparents around the country afraid to answer their telephones. There are childless couples who cower in basements at the first sound of small shoes crunching up the driveway. There are single people who have stopped answering the door. Kindly uncles have taken to rising at 3:00 A.M. to carry out the garbage. Favourite aunts leave for work before light, come home after dark. Whatever it takes to avoid getting hit up yet again.

There is no more room in their kitchens for boxes of gawdawful cookies. They prefer garbage bags that hold. They don't believe in light bulbs that will still be working long after the sun's burnt out. And, on top of all that, they're beginning to realize that having a "nice" reputation around the neighbourhood is an expensive luxury.

At first it just seems like a few $2 pledges here and there, $5 if you happen to be related or live right next door, $10 if you're unfortunate enough to be a grandparent, a kindly uncle, or a favourite aunt, but eventually the T-ball and five-pitch and gymnastics and soccer and swimming and rope jumping and skating and a thousand other activities add up to what used to be a reasonable annual income.

Just look down the street on any given weekend. At the end of the driveway, pacing anxiously, you will notice the Modern Parent. The nervous kid reluctantly heading up your driveway is signed up in one or more of the above activities, and it is time, obviously, to collect the loot from all those who were hit up a month or so earlier when the parent came home with a completed registration form, a receipt for a good deal of money, and a glossy pledge form that the child was not to hand in until all the blank spaces were filled with the names of a dozen people who had, up until this moment, been sitting around wondering how on earth they could buy some dreadful cookies even the dog won't eat.

These "supporters" and "sponsors" – if they happen to answer the doorbell – will find it hard to say no because, of course, the money is going toward a good, healthy activity. The money from these cookies, for example, will be used to buy brand-new bases for the T-ball kids, even though no kid in the history of T-ball has ever known what bases are for, new or old. Money will go toward hiring real umpires for the five-pitch the eight-year-old girls are playing, even though 99 per cent of the umpire's job will involve retrieving missed balls for the catcher. Money will go toward providing each and every kid who plays with a trophy at the end of the season, though no kid will ever have the slightest reason why he or she was handed this prize. Money will go toward out-of-town trips for hockey teams where, after travelling seven hours by automobile and booking into the hotel, they will discover they will be playing against teams that also came seven hours by car – from exactly the same city.

How has it come to this?

If everyone automatically wins a trophy, what will happen if something special ever happens? Have the Modern Parents done such an effective job of usurping play that they are now turning children into just another piece of equipment in the game of parental involvement?

The bags must be new, the bats brand new, the balls snow white, the accredited, paid umpire in place, adults strategically placed about the base paths, adults keeping score, and the trophies on order. Everything perfect so that the eight-year-old can come up to bat, flail away, and pray silently that she won't make contact and have to figure out which way to run and what it all means if she should happen to get there.

Questions such as these the adults gathered can hardly wait to answer. But they are questions that can be just as easily answered without a paid umpire, brand spanking-new equipment – and pledges to collect at the end of the game.

School Days

On the eve of March Break, in a small public school on the outskirts of Ottawa, two nervous grade five students moved to the microphone, the fourteenth act out of the twenty-one that would make up a typical school's annual "Talent Night." They were listed as the Singing Friends, and, accompanied by their teacher on a nearby piano, they managed a charming, if not exactly crowd-stopping, version of a 1980s hit, "That's What Friends Are For."

No one would argue that the song is anything but hopelessly sentimental, but no one could deny that the effect was real. Whether it was the lines – "And if I should ever go away/ Well then close your eyes/ And try and feel the way we do today" – or just the image of two eleven-year-old girls staring at each other as they sang, one member of the audience wanted them to know that she, anyway, had been moved to tears.

Perhaps it was the contrast between the sentiment and

the situation. One of the Singing Friends has known three different school gymnasiums in less than four years. Such is the suburban school experience, forever fluid, of the modern day.

This struck home a few days later in a small town several hours away through the Ontario bush. Four of the same children who had been in the school gymnasium now sat in a small living room staring at a picture that seemed to them to have come from another century. And once they had it explained to them, they thought it from another planet, as well.

The picture, black-and-white and blown up to ridiculous proportions, belongs to a man who began school in 1953 by simply walking down the street with his two best friends. Thirty-four years later, his two best friends are exactly the same people. Not only that, but while the four modern schoolchildren stared suspiciously, two of those 1953 originals were able to move their fingers down the three rows of black-and-white children and tell, virtually head by head, where each classmate was today and what had happened to them.

For today's kids, the class pictures from two years and two schools back are already filled with the faces of strangers. But for the three friends who walked down to Mrs. Robinson's class that September day of 1953, there was only one school and one continuous experience, though the moments most easily recalled involve bloodied noses, detentions, expulsions, and a teenaged hockey riot in the next town that would easily rival the lights-out battle of the Canadian and Soviet juniors in the world championship. The experience covers first and last cigarettes, first (and in one case last) drinks, and it remains homes where you neither knock nor call ahead.

It means when Randolph Scott died, a bit of all three passed on as well.

It seems on the surface so ridiculously quaint – the three still calling each other on birthdays, the three posing again and again for a silly arm-about-the-shoulders photo that was first taken when all were eight and all had hair – but the whole story is not always quaint at all. Thirty-four years could not pass without the usual trauma, family and personal and even legal, perhaps even more trauma than average, but certainly not more troubles than friendship is worth.

Under today's circumstances and entirely on the surface, these three friends might not appear to have all that much in common – one man drives horses in a timber operation, one sells clothes, one has a newspaper column – but there is a bond there that, if it has held through all of this, will find holding to the end a breeze.

Thirty-four years is not all that long ago, but it does belong to that time and that place when other students never seemed to go anywhere, not even to Florida for March Break.

And though much has improved in the school system in the years since that photograph was taken, it is difficult not to wish – particularly at a moment when two eleven-year-olds look each other in the eye and promise friendship forever – that in certain cases today's children would not have to be given more opportunities than their parents ever had.

It is difficult not to wish for them simply the same chance kids used to have, the opportunity to get to know someone well enough and long enough for life.

❄

God only knows how such thoughts find their way into the brain, but we have all asked ourselves what we would grab if the house was on fire, everyone was safe, and there was time only for one quick armful on the way out.

You can always get a new television, and they can always send out new bills, but think about it – what would you grab?

I used to think it would be the row of photo albums that will soon fill a shelf against the near wall, a dozen glossy books stuffed with the history of this family told from the point of view of the one who controls the camera.

It is the most curious account of the modern Canadian family. For one thing, it is almost always summer. For another, people are always smiling. Children sit happily at pianos, fish flail helplessly at the end of lines, birds land constantly on tiny, outstretched hands – the sum of our perfect days set off by a hundred perfect sunsets.

But what if instead we had thought to grab something else? Something like the school journals.

No one seems to know where these little journals originated, but all parents know they did not have them when they were at school. All we have to remember our schooldays by are class pictures and report cards, both of which require a wince to look at again. But the school journal – those little blue and yellow and orange and pink exercise books, usually cut in half, that come home in the school bag every three months or so – they surely are a far more endearing, and often more accurate, remembrance of things past.

Sitting in front of me is history on the run by four different children, and it is shocking how little resemblance it bears to the glossy memories on the shelf. For every photograph of a perfect weekend trip these journals hold at least one graphically illustrated drawing of the road kill that made the trip worthwhile.

To counter the photo of the happy family setting out in the canoe, there is, somewhere in the pile, a counter rendering of the fishing trip: a kid bawling his eyes out, the balloon above his screeching head filled with "LIAR! SHATUP! NYA NYA NYA!!"

It requires more work to go through the journals. One must, for example, know that "sllypotr" spells "sleepover" and "byoutifl" is the official grade-two spelling for "beautiful." But the rewards are well worth while.

In the drawings of me, for example, I have full heads of curling black hair – which is far more accurate than anything that can be found in the photo albums. I am also very large and very strong. And what I thought was a boring weekend in Toronto was actually a trip "right around the wrld." Not to mention the farm we own in some place called "Sekachewon."

According to the journals of record, these children love going to the dentist, judo, piano lessons, school. But there are other surprises as well. If you went by the photographs, you would think that smiling came easily. If you went by the journals, you would know: "Today is pitchrs and I rilly lookd stuped because I dont know how to smile."

And what was, to you, nothing but a quick walk in the park – clouded over, no use even taking the camera – becomes, in a journal, something tour operators could package and sell: *The trail has fox holes. last year we made a trap. we put a hol lot of branches over a fox hole. We also made a*

bridg over a stream and we also climbd a big steep hill and we
were water sking at the sand pit and we tride to find salmanders
but we culdnt find eny because the dirt was to dry and then we
dug tunals in the soft sand. we made chairs but they all brock and
we made a table but the table did not work so we did without. i
wonder if we will do it again this year. i hope it will be as fun as
last year.

Just try framing that in a 50-mm lens.

First whiff of smoke, I know what I'm taking with me.

It is the month of the annual school science fairs, the time of the year when certain adults are forced to stumble in absolute bewilderment from booth to booth through a school gymnasium.

At each stop the routine is the same: listen patiently to the explanation, gamely try out a simple experiment, congratulate and thank the participant – and then stumble on in a daze, not having understood a blessed thing.

Perhaps it is time non-scientific parents came out of the closet. Their fear of ridicule, after all, would be called irrational. But since, of course, it would be called irrational by a scientifically trained mind, it would be of little comfort to those who are so afflicted.

Some people grow up and never learn to ride a bicycle. Some cannot swim. Others cannot sing. But the ones you never hear about – the ones most in need of support groups – are those, and I am among them, who are missing that part of the brain that deals with science.

Now, if you understand how soap works, you will not understand how demeaning, humiliating, embarrassing this can be to someone who is normal in all other ways. But if you do not understand how soap works, you will know first-hand the cruelty of the situation.

Think about it: they do not hold hockey fairs where you could stand around and discuss the Pittsburgh Penguins with your kid and the principal. They do not hold outdoor fairs where you can show off your vast knowledge of the Madawaska River or your photos of the Prairies. They don't even hold VCR fairs where you could at least talk about last year's movies.

No, they hold science fairs, and you find you are suddenly standing in front of a Bristol-board booth while a grade-four student loses you completely on the negative poles of an electromagnet. And you are no sooner out of that than you find yourself in front of a grade-six kid who snorts with derision as you try, unsuccessfully, to blow two hanging ping-pong balls apart.

They think you are being kind, standing there listening so patiently. What they don't know is that you haven't understood a single word since they began their spiel.

The fact of the matter is that you won't carry a single new piece of information with you when you finally break free of the gymnasium doors and are allowed to return to the sort of scientific knowledge you are comfortable with:

• A car requires gas and a key.
• It is raining because the man on the radio predicted it would.
• A television works when you plug it in and turn it on.
• A refrigerator's temperature is controlled by a dial.
• You can only eat and drink so much.

People with scientific minds cannot possibly understand the anxiety those of us without such tools live under. We are more frightened of garage mechanics than dentists. We prefer toys to be destroyed rather than broken. How can we be expected to worry about nuclear leaks when we don't understand why electricity doesn't leak out of the wall outlets? We will go to our graves wondering how soap works.

But before we get there, we will suffer through the same recurring nightmare. Somehow, you have been sent back through time. But unlike The Connecticut Yankee in King Arthur's Court, you are not suddenly blessed with a single insight into what the future holds.

In 1880 you tell them that one day there will be airplanes in the sky, and someone will want to know how they work.

In 1500 you tell them that they have electricity to look forward to, and someone will ask what it is.

In Biblical times you tell them about steam power, and they will ask for a demonstration.

In prehistoric time, you happen to mention fire, and pass the rest of your miserable days rubbing two sticks together while they point and laugh.

It is our shame. It is something we hide as we stand by a grade-five booth and understand one word out of every seven on aerodynamics, knowing that a nod is the only response possible each time the budding young scientist makes eye contact. We can only thank God – or whatever's out there in the total unknown – that the science fair comes only once a year.

❋

For politicians, the one word that never fails to boil the blood is "credibility." But for the Modern Parent the most difficult word in the English language is "satisfactory."

It is a word that has lost its meaning, just as today's parents have lost their senses.

It happens with the arrival home of the term report card, that disturbing moment when the Modern Parents finally recognize that what they most want out of this life is for their own children to turn into the very students they once despised, sucking up at every opportunity, fingers snapping at every question. You know who I'm talking about – the typical, average Canadian parent, the one who is able to say "We only want you to give your best effort," with all the sincerity of a minor league hockey coach saying, "It's not whether you win or lose, it's how you play the game that counts."

Kids know what really counts in both school and sports: the score. And they also know that while it might not matter to them whether they win or lose, it sure as heck matters to Mom and Dad and the coach. After all, they're the ones *really* playing the game, and the object of any meaningful test is to take the opposition, which in the case of school marks turns out not to be the other kids as much as it is the other parents.

That, of course, is because today's parents are less interested in raising children than they are in wearing them, and so any comment – from a goal on the rink to an "A" in the classroom – is far more a measure of proper parenting than it ever is of how the child might be doing.

Scientists do not yet understand the genetic breakdown of this recent phenomenon, but there is no longer much doubt that parents who describe themselves as average are now capable of producing only above-average children. That is why in today's schools there are no longer average students, but rather those who are in enrichment, those who need enrichment, and those who aren't in enrichment because the stupid system hasn't been able to track down – and fix – the learning disability. Once they get the bugs worked out of the system, the Canadian educational system should be returning an endless string of Nobel laureates to these typical – but deserving – parents.

But first, there's work to do. There has to be a more satisfactory report card measure than "satisfactory," for example. Most dictionaries are sadly out of date on this word, defining it as "convincing" and "adequate" when even the most average Modern Parent knows that it now means "utterly hopeless."

Report cards, as today's typical parents have come to know, are written almost entirely in code. With "satis-factory" clearly listed below "excellent," it is obvious that "satisfactory" can only mean that the teacher – not the child – is failing to live up to the parents' expecta-tions. Average parents also know that the "Teacher's Comments" section is composed in two separate lan-guages, one designed to lull the parents into a state of inaction, the other to be entered into the official school records – undoubtedly dooming the child forever. For example, if the teacher writes that the child "is coming along quite well," the more astute average parent will know to ask: Coming along from what? And "well" in this case means "barely adequate," suggesting that, unless the parent immediately takes this before the school board, the child in question could be painted with a "satisfactory" brush for the rest of his or her life.

The rest of the coding is even more complicated. Typical parents understand, of course, that an "A" is a sincere compliment to them and a "C" or less is a clear indication that the teacher has it in for the child. The most important of all, however, is the key phrase "Greater Effort Required," which today's typical parent immediately recognizes for what it is. Usually disguised in a cluster of other phrases such as "sloppy printing" or "short attention span," the parents who ultimately pass will know that "Greater Effort Required," is not aimed at the one who carries the report card home, but at the one who sends it back.

And that is why some Modern Parents will be spending more on the teacher's Christmas present this year than they will on the kids'.

Lost and Found

*I*t's a word that means nothing to most of us, everything to so many. *Homestead.* They don't use the word – not as a noun, never as a verb - in Scarborough highrises or Surrey townhouses, but out here in Saskatchewan this most Canadian of words echoes on in this most Canadian of provinces. Out here it comes from a prayer book rather than the dictionary.

Homestead. The word you can pass to others easily. What it means is another matter.

Somewhere back down the maternal line, the four Ontario city children out running along the gravel lane come from here, but they do not know that. When they have asked where they come from, they have had new hospitals pointed out to them. When they are asked where they come from, they give an address with a postal code.

They do not understand that the first letters to arrive at this homestead were addressed to the "North-West Territories." They were sent before Saskatchewan became a province in 1905. They came from a small town in England and they were filled with unstated worry over the terrible things that would surely follow a young man's mad dream to head out to a new country and a new life.

The four Ontario city children come in for breakfast. They want sugar-coated cereal. They pay no attention to the box of carefully tied letters that sits at the near end of the long kitchen table. Inside the box is their own history. The letters the young man sent back home the moment his ship docked at St. John's, the story of the storm, the icebergs, the way passengers were "penned together like pigs" and how they either behaved "like fighting cocks" at mealtime or went without. There are letters about work on the Grand Trunk Railway, letters about work on a farm that began at 5:00 A.M. and ended at 8:00 P.M., and one lovely letter mentions a certain "miss" he has met, nothing more.

If the letters are all put together, a novel emerges. The miss returns to England with plans to save up, come back and marry. Her family disapproves. The letters from Canada are cut off. A sympathetic aunt intervenes and acts as a go-between between the young letter writers. Somewhere in the pile is a postcard with a deliciously cryptic message: "Do not fail in your mission." Years pass and the miss finally books passage back to Canada, never to return to England. The meat of a novel, but it happens to be true.

Most of us are not so fortunate. We can point to the bush, name a city, figure there was probably a name changed somewhere along the line, but few can pick up their past from a cupboard shelf.

The kids race to play in the empty granaries. They pass over, and do not notice, the hollow in the ground

where the sod hut stood for so long and where an aunt
and uncle were born. They run to see where the chickens
were kept, and do not stop for the old plough that rests,
bone-dry, in the willows. They would not believe that
the job now done so casually in an air-conditioned tractor was once done by a single man, sweating and stum-
bling, with the reins over his shoulders and a tired horse
ahead. The kids run along a field of bright yellow rape.
They marvel at how far they can see. They think the land
came cleared. In one old building the first tractor sits on
studded steel wheels. In another, the old "Royal
Favourite" stove is rusting. They are more interested in
the swallows' nests under the eaves.

In the nearest town there is a pioneer museum with
the clothes and tools of the man and woman who sailed
from England. The kids wonder what time the swimming pool opens. In the town's cemetery there is a small
tombstone to the couple that once were so young
together and who died within months of each other,
their English accents surviving seventy-five years in the
new country in which others expected they wouldn't
last very long. There never seems time to visit.

How, you wonder, can you ever get this across to kids
who, a few days earlier, sat in a prairie cafe staring in
wonder at something that came from a past they could
not comprehend? A jukebox. It is the dilemma of all
who move, whether from England in 1905 or Italy in
1955 or Vietnam in 1985. We all have to come from
somewhere and, somewhere down the line, we all forget
exactly where. Force the point, and you're certain to fail
in your mission.

Best just to let it be and hope that, on a hot Saskatchewan evening, you come across a very young girl stand-

ing in a bedroom staring at old photographs of people she will never meet but should know.

"What are you looking for?"

"Nothing," she says, and leaves quickly, as if startled by someone she didn't expect to be there.

Whatever became of the Sunday drive?

For two weekends now, ever since a young mother wondered out loud where it had gone to, I have been watching for signs that the Sunday drive still exists. Certainly, it is beyond debate that cars are still among us, that roads still lead off to nowhere in particular, that they still make ice cream, and that Sunday, at least for the time being, is still a day of rest. And it is also true that, on any given Sunday, cars can still be found heading out unfamiliar roads, in search of whatever happens. But the young mother is right: it is no longer the same.

The cars that now slow sharply at a crossroads in search of the road least taken contain old people, a small white-haired couple or two elderly women who seem more like accessories to their small, sensible vehicles than driver and passenger. Not young families in search of singing frogs or crabapples or a quiet place along the river where the sun stays hot on the rocks that are too large to throw in, but old people whose own families should be off on their own meaningless escapes, but aren't for the simple reason that there is no longer time for the Sunday drive.

That is not to say that cars filled with short, spring-loaded necks are not to found on the highways come Sunday, just to say that they move with intention rather than speculation. They maintain a steady speed rather than braking without warning. They turn when they're supposed to, and never – as those other Sunday cars do – by shooting past the turn, pulling over, thinking about it, pulling an illegal U-turn and coming back like a cat that thinks it might have seen something move in the bushes. They hurry because they have places to go. There are practices to make, demonstrations to cheer, classes to take, small friends – who have been called ahead and booked – to visit.

The days when everyone moped around the house until someone had the brilliant inspiration to go for a ride – and everyone else was instantly available – are long past. Of course, so too are cars that always had room, if not belts and neck supports, for a few extra little bodies if friends happened to be moping around with nothing to do as well, and not due at 2:45 P.M. for a recital and then again at 3:30 P.M. for a light workout in preparation for next week's tournament which, of course, will rule out next Sunday as well . . .

Too bad, for let us pause for a moment and remember what they're missing.

Will they never destroy an entire set of clothes on a sloping gravel pit? Will they never stand and stare at an abandoned farm and wonder how people ever lived there and what on earth their kids ever did for fun? Will they never sit of an early evening at the side of a swamp and wonder if there is a creature on Earth quite so gross and loud as the common toad? Will they never know that ice cream eaten on a strange village street has an entirely different flavour to that eaten in a familiar suburb? Will they never know that there are treasures like spruce cones and pussywillows and flat stones that aren't sold in fifty-cent packages at Mac's and require a $3.95 official book to store them in? And will they never, then, know the bittersweet pleasure of growing up and heading out themselves with a new young family in search of those roads where the finest moments imaginable lie just around the next turn – and if not there, then the turn after that?

Never, if they never get there now.

They deserve to be taken out – even if it means cancelling something that is vital and necessary in the endless drive to turn them into successful, fully formed, perfect human beings. They should be taken out, if only to see the Sunday cars wandering happily lost along the back roads, Sunday cars filled with people old enough to be their grandparents. Sunday cars filled with old people looking for nothing in part, but still capable of finding something that may one day be lost to us all.

The single, scribbled piece of note paper clings to the refrigerator like a message that has somehow slipped through a time warp.

"Brownies," the note reminds. "Same time, same place. 50¢."

Fifty cents.

It sticks to the refrigerator door beside another note that speaks for the times – "Mom owes me $10" – and is within fluttering distance of a calendar that proves, once again, why September has been downright sadistic when compared to April, the cruellest month. September and the return to school teach us that, if the prime minister truly had the best interests of this country in mind, he would have matched the $6.3-billion day care promise with a $6.3-billion program to bail out families whose children have grown out of diapers and into Ocean Pacific. But it is not just the fact that everyone else seems to be wearing Ralph Lauren Polo and Roots to school while you try, yet another fall, to argue the impossible: that the only difference between what K–Mart or an older sister offers and what the other kids are wearing is a silly, meaningless label. It is so much more than that.

It costs, they say, $1,000 to outfit a kid for hockey. If he makes the competitive team, triple that and throw in a new station wagon and the cost of a marriage break-down to boot. Another thousand or more for skiing. A few hundred dollars more for gymnastics, horse riding, swimming, figure skating, music. A few tens for ballet, tap dancing, judo, baton. And add to that sum so many ones and twos that they soon total into the hundreds – no thousands, *billions* – for the treats that must be tagged on to each event just so they will put on their outfit and head, screaming and fighting and kicking and crying, out the door to enjoy themselves.

"Brownies. Same time. Same place. 50¢."

At night, when they are finally asleep and the steam is still coming off the credit card, I light candles and place them on each side of the refrigerator, kneel down where the Tahiti Treat has turned the floor to a cushion of Krazy Glue, stare up at this simple, lovely message and pray that the madness will one day pass.

In the local paper there is an announcement that another Girl Guide company has folded "due to the lack of adult volunteers." This should come as no surprise: those adults who are not busy driving the car pool to gymnastics are at their second jobs, desperate to make sure the next post-dated cheque for jazz dancing will not bounce, as the last one did, and the one before that.

There is no car pool required for Brownies. They walk, the way children once did in a far-off time and a far-off place to hockey rinks. There are no parents standing around with growing frowns, wondering whether or not they are getting their money's worth or whether the coach has something personal against their kid. But the benefits do not end there.

Does karate offer a law that orders the kids to be "cheerful and obedient" and think "of other people before herself"? Does hockey have secret signs and handshakes? (This could prove invaluable should the child move through Tweenies and Brownies and Guides and on, one day, to federal politics.) Does ballet have a "Grand Howl"? What better preparation for children who might one day grow up (grow sideways?) into journalists? Does tap dancing have a "flying up ceremony" that can prepare young Canadians for one day being appointed to the Senate? And where else, I ask you, do they give out badges for walking the dog and doing the laundry and keeping your room tidy for two weeks?

Just check the first three requisites for the home portion of the Golden Bar. "Set a table for a meal. Help to wash the dishes. Leave the kitchen tidy." All this, for nothing more than a pin to stick above your left pocket.

"Brownies. Same time. Same place. 50¢."

It's a wonder we don't stuff the credit card into her belt purse, just out of habit.

The Dog

*I*t is always disconcerting to discover that the voice at the other end of the line belongs to the police – all the more so to learn that they are calling about one of yours.

"We have your dog here at the station."

For a long moment I am speechless, and the OPP constable mistakes the silence for denial. He recites the numbers of a licence, but they mean nothing.

"It's registered in your name, sir." But still I am speechless.

"Black and brown with a little white, fairly small – is that yours, sir?"

It certainly sounds like her, but how? The dog is nearly fourteen years old, has not only never before crossed the law but these days can barely cross the lawn. It would seem more reasonable if the police were calling about one of the kids being caught in a bank hold-up, or if the Pinto had turned itself in as a menace to public safety. But we are speaking here of the totally harmless, a mongrel that came free of charge from up a nearly forgotten street. It came to the door in the hands of a dirty-faced kid who'd been told by his mother to get rid of them or else, and we took one in one of those weak moments that seem to follow puppies around like paper towels.

The vet was diplomatic. "I wouldn't expect much if I were you."

We did not and were pleasantly surprised. If anything the dog was too dependable. The unimpressed vet had thought it might be a beagle, but time produced something quite different, and the dog's insistance on continually rounding up children meant that she came to be called a borderline collie.

Like everyone's dog, she had certain special traits – including a strange ability to remove peanuts from the shell – but still, just a dog. After fourteen years, you take them for granted. No one noticed that the puppy gagging on the end of a leash had not broken away on her own for more than a decade. The vets look at them and mention grizzled muzzles or cloudy eyes, but you see only the pup that first came knocking at the door.

But then, one day you see what time has done. For this particular dog it happened recently on a long walk through the woods to an abandoned farm the kids are convinced they can buy and fix up for less than forty cents. Halfway in, the dog lay down panting and simply refused to move. The only way to get her in the mile or so was to carry her like a baby. When we reached the destination, I carried her inside in search of shade, unfortunately walking straight into a large porcupine coming down the gutted stairwell. Porcupine and person both panicked, but all the dog did was turn slightly in my arms, bark twice, and growl, baring teeth the vet says are desperately in need of proper care.

The porcupine ran for the door but the person won, still carrying the dog like a small baby. As I bolted over the broken doors, she tucked her head under my arm and snarled as if she somehow had the porcupine on the run.

Perhaps from her perspective it seemed that way. After all, her legs never moved and the porcupine did indeed fade into the distance. The dog had obviously won the day.

But not with those who mattered. Following that collapse in the woods, it was clear that no one expected much anymore. Everyone agreed that fourteen years was a long time – ninety-eight, the more mathematical kids said, in dog years – and from that moment on she was treated as if the glory days were forever gone. After that sad day in the woods, no one even suggested another walk.

"*Sir?*"

"Yes? Yes, the dog's mine, all right. I'll be right down."

She was sitting at the back of the station near the garage doors, two young officers sitting with her, each with a hand ruffling up and down her back.

"She's never run away before?" the youngest one asked.

"Never."

"Well, we found her running along the road up there. Shaking like a leaf."

"Never seen a dog so nervous," the other officer said. "I wonder what got into her?"

"I don't know," I said.

But later, watching her dance in the seat on the way home, I did know.

It wasn't nervousness, but excitement. And what got into her was what should get into us all when they write us off before our time.

My father and my dog are about the same age, 82 and 16, though some will argue that those dog years work out – on a scale of seven man years to the dog year – to more like 112. That doesn't seem possible. After all, how many 112-year-olds do you see driving around with their heads stuck out the window?

The point is, my father and my dog are both getting on. They're both crystal clear in the head but stiff in the morning. The man hears much better than the dog, but the dog doesn't have the bad limp the man has had since he was hit by a lumber truck several years ago. Yet no one – my mother, on certain occasions, excepted – has ever suggested we have my father put down. The dog is another matter.

For months now, every time a quiet moment and a well-meaning friend or relative present themselves at the same time, the topic comes up: What are you going to do about Bumps? They don't mean when are we going to have her toenails clipped. They mean, plain and simple, *when are you going to kill her?*

I never know what to answer. It is no longer, in this day and age, a question of loading up the rifle and walking off into the woods together for an hour or so and then coming back alone. (Who on earth could handle that?) All you have to do in the Modern Age is drive up, walk the dog in, hand over the leash to someone in a white coat, kneel down, pet the poor beast, hand over your Visa card and then take home a story about the dog going to sleep and being a lot happier for it.

Kids don't buy that. If it's so great for the dog, why is everyone bawling? But once the thought is there, it becomes part of every decision.

The dog picks up a temporary bladder problem. Do you kill the dog just because it can't help piddling on the rug?

You have a long vacation coming up. The dog doesn't travel well anymore. Do you "put it out of its misery" just because it has never before been put in a kennel? How can you? And though she shook like a leaf when we pushed her into the kennel, her tail was still wagging when we got back.

We took her to the lake for a weekend, the same lake where, in another time, she would leap from the vehicle and be off the end of the dock before the first kid hit the water. Now she must be carried from the car seat to the ground and lifted from the ground up the steps to the cabin. Out for a quick moment one dark night, she became disoriented and fell off the rocks by the dock. There being no light, she could not see shore. There being no life to her ears, she could not hear the calls. She headed straight out into the black night until, in a reversal of the old roles, I had to leap in after her and herd her back to shore.

Last week it seemed the decision might be taken for us. There was something growing on her that wasn't right. The vet could cut it out, he said, but at her age she might not wake up from the anesthetic. So be it, we said, and said good-bye just in case.

And while we waited, the older kids got out an old photo album with a black and white puppy inside that looks like a laundered fuzzball where today there are only stubborn mats and a lingering smell. They wished they had her now like she was then. So do we all. So does the old dog that still quivers and runs in her sleep.

The youngest girl told her class and at recess a boy she barely knows came up and offered to help her pray.

The vet did not call with bad news. At the end of the day the tail was once again trying to wag, but she couldn't stand up and had to be carried everywhere. The kids brought her water and blankets and lay down with their heads against hers, talking in low voices about matters between them, while against the wall stood the adults who must one day decide, telling themselves that the moment it's clear she's in pain or can't get up on her back legs or . . .

Convincing themselves that they will have the common sense to act, for in a world that is filled with such stark reality and inhumanity, this is, after all, only a dog.

Recently I drove out into the countryside to pick up the middle daughter from a weekend sleepover. Her stuff was piled by the door and, like any trusting parent, I quickly went through the pile to find out how much of what she'd taken with her was going to be coming home.

- Pajamas. *Check.*
- A change of clothes. *Check.*
- Stuffed toy. *Check.*
- Toothbrush. *Check.*

• Dog dish . . .

I can see where this is going to take some explaining.

The facts of life finally caught up to our sixteen-year-old mutt. Sure Bumps was stone deaf. Yes, her fur *was* matted. Indeed, she did stink. I think, too, she had dog's Alzheimer's. How else do you explain things like constantly getting caught under chairs and not being able to figure out that her chain led straight back to the door? But did that mean we should kill her?

We talked about it. We edged up to the ugly act when she temporarily lost control of her bodily fluids, but who in God's name could put a dog down because it piddled on a carpet? We came close when she had to have that growth removed from her rear end, but when she came out of the anaesthetic with that once magnificent tail still wagging, who could not hope for the impossible? Everyone knows that the fate of a mongrel is a poor measure against human lives being lost and gained, but then . . . well, the only way to understand is to go through it yourself, and to know that there are certain things measured within a family that are not intended to make sense beyond. Outside of the family involved, a pet's death is, at best, a pause in the conversation. But within, it has a lasting expression one will not find in conversation of any length.

"You will know when the time has come," we were told. And it was true. First there was a second growth, this time inoperable. Then she fell down the stairs and couldn't get up. Her back end was gone.

And yet, the last day I came home and she was still there, she tried to do the only chore that has ever been expected of her: whip a bushy tail from side to side and act as if my coming through the front door was the most significant event that had ever taken place. But she still couldn't move.

The family had a talk. It didn't go well.

The moon was full on the drive to the vet's, full and large and the colour of a yellow apple.

Vets are good at these things. You're welcome to come in. You're welcome to stay. You're encouraged to hang on. And you do. But you know you can't hang on forever.

It's over very quickly, very quietly. It would be a lie to say it feels good but it does feel right. Just as they said it would.

Back home her last tracks were still in the front yard, and, for once, you pray for snow.

You deal with the tears and turn to putting away things where every sound – a dropped chain, a rattled collar – sends ghosts scurrying about the house, some coming down the stairs to greet you, some wanting out, some two years old again and jumping as high as the worn leash can be held.

That first night, when there is no one to let out, there seems no way to close off the day. But one child has gone to bed early. One has an envelope of black-and-white matted hair. One has an old collar on her dresser. And one, of course, is found sleeping with a dog dish.

You know then that it will take much more than snow to cover the tracks.

And even if it doesn't feel good, it does, somehow, feel right.

You don't have to sit on the Supreme Court to know it's not right to keep your children locked up in a steel cage. But that's what has happened in our house. And all I can do is trust that the authorities who look into sick situations will give me a chance to explain.

Let's go back a couple of weeks to the earliest hints of what was to come.

First the snow melted away, and when the front yard emerged it brought with it an old dog chain that had rusted solid. It had lain where it had been dropped that snowy day last December when we finally recognized that there was no use pretending a very old, very sick mutt could be put out and come back in with her hearing back, eyes sharp, and rear end under control.

Only a day or so after the rusted chain showed up, a glossy dog book was found on the kitchen table. Then came the tours of the pet shops, which eventually evolved into a running contest to discover which store had the most gall. The pet stores, it turns out, are leading the western world in the art of re-packaging.

Say ten years ago you had a poodle who went into heat and took off on the lam with the neighbourhood spaniel. A few weeks later you probably would have put an ad in the local paper saying "Puppies: poodle and spaniel mix, free to good home" and hoped for the best. But not now. What the pet stores do now is invent new breeds and flog them for the price of a used car.

The offspring of the poodle that ran off with the spaniel are now marketed as "spoodles," but there are also "cock-a-poos" and "terri-poos" and, for all we know "Great Poos" – all of which only goes to prove that a poodle running loose is even more loose than anyone ever imagined.

You can't find what you're looking for in the classifieds or the pound. But then, one day, you come home from work and there, standing over a water bowl like a toddler at the edge of a swimming pool, is a little black and white mess that looks – unbelievably – as if it has everything *but* poodle in it. An enterprising pet store would probably call it a "Great St. Bulcolbeagolretzer," put up a price tag of $475 and have to limit them to one per customer. But this one came, as the best dogs do, from a farm, for free, a friend doing a favour.

It has been seventeen years since a puppy has been around. Back then we foolishly used to tell people a puppy was just as much trouble as a baby, but then four babies came along and we conveniently forgot we had ever been so stupid. But now that we've forgotten how awful new babies are, we're back being stupid. A puppy is at least as much trouble as a baby.

With babies, it was not necessary to have newspapers all over the floor – and where there are not newspapers there are yellow puddles and much worse. Babies didn't chew the furniture, bite every passing cuff. This thing is four weeks old and already there are children afraid to come into the house.

Who could have ever predicted such good luck!

But even our own small children are under seige. So someone went out and got a steel cage, just to make sure that no one ever came home to discover the television had been eaten. Only no one had the guts to put the creature in and lock it up.

And that's why, right now, a metal cage filled with children is sitting in the middle of the living-room floor. They have crawled in there to watch television in peace. They sit, their cuffs and fingers and toes drawn tight to their bodies, while outside a four-week-old puppy of unknown origins stalks back and forth, pausing only to piddle where there is no newspaper.

Holidays

Ah the Great Outdoors. You just can't beat 'em. And here's why:

Let us begin today's vacation on the road, say Highway 17 leading north from Wawa.

You have just passed a large sign saying something like "Gas Supplies Uncertain for next 4,567,239 kilometres." Ever responsible, you check, noting that you have almost a quarter-tank left. And on you speed into oblivion.

You have to speed. Evening is falling and you have no idea whatsoever where you will be spending the night.

"I don't feel so good," comes a small voice from the back.

"You'll be alright."

On and on you hurtle through the spruce, the vehicle filled with the unmistakeable sounds of summer.

"Can't you read a map?"

"I spilled my pop."

"Are we there yet?"

"How far do we have to count?"

"Is this Saskatchewan?"

"I don't feel so good."

"Just hang on a little longer, okay?"

On you charge, with night falling almost as fast as the gas needle, on past motels more frightening than the bush, on past what may have been the last available campsite on the face of this Earth. You should have turned, but you didn't turn. It's not your fault. It's never your fault.

"I don't feel so good."

"You'll be alright."

And then, suddenly, like the arrival of the cavalry, like Gretzky on a breakaway, a small yellow provincial park sign looms.

Yes, there is space.

Down you go, the clean vehicle vanishing in the dust, kids and pop and cameras airborne from the washboard.

"I-I d-d-don't-t f-feel so g-g-g-good."

But you, you feel terrific. You, after all, have found the perfect spot. Just as you are unhitching and unpacking and unloading, four kids come flying down the path screaming that *they* have found the most perfect campsite in history. It is perfectly level. There is a free block of wood on the fire. It is near the water. There are no mosquitoes. People who sleep there will never grow old.

And so, beaten down by reason and decibel count, you move. Night falling, and you hitch everything up again and drag it all down the path three sites closer to the washrooms.

You unhitch the camper. You pull out the tent. You put up the camper, level it, and run the extension cord out and over to the plug so someone will be able to play

Bon Jovi later and drown out the loons. The extension cord, however, comes up three feet short.

Down goes the camper, on goes the hitch, back goes the vehicle, curse goes the driver, but eventually the camper is close enough for stereo and the process can begin again from scratch.

Up goes the tent, momentarily. A catch rips and down goes the tent, rather more temporarily.

The mosquitoes have found us.

Fortunately, knowing the outdoors like the backs of our eyelids, we are more than prepared, for we have packed civilization's latest invention: small cans of citronella fuel complete with wicks. One can, however, has no wick. The other lights, but is so sensitive to wind it blows out at the first brush of a mosquito's wing.

"I don't feel so good."

"*Who cares?*"

The first rotation of children hit the camper, all pushing and falling into the same bed, the one opposite the hitch, the side that tips if too many people get on one side and nobody's on the other . . .

A kid cuts her finger on a can.

The wood the park supplies is so green it has to be split into feathers, doused with naphtha, and struck dead-on with a space laser. But eventually it does catch, and the smoke that twists above the pitchy wood seems somehow to have insulted the mosquitoes to the point that they have stomped off to other campsites. And the kid who didn't feel good has crawled, without prodding, into his sleeping bag and is already fast asleep.

The fire snaps with pitch, the tapes are turned off, and a loon calls from far out over the water. The moon is out. Soon it will be full. The stars have depth here and make things like mortgages and careers so inconsequential in comparison that they are not even worthy of consideration on a night like this. An owl asks more pertinent questions from a nearby tree.

And this – a quiet hour while the coals burn down – is what the Great Outdoors is all about.

In the morning, the sun is bright and warm and all continues well until you finish packing and pull out and happen to glance down at the gas gauge. The needle has just entered the "E" zone. And there is nothing on the horizon but more spruce.

You don't feel so good.

But don't worry, by the end of the day you'll be all right again. Guaranteed.

About an hour ago we crossed back into Ontario after a week camping through the northern United States and another week before that in the Canadian Prairies. The customs officer simply held her nose with one hand and waved us through with the other. Another day and we will be home. And once we get there, it will be time to begin the Kodak Adjustment of this year's summer vacation.

You know what I mean. It's a bit like the way the Chinese rewrite history. You take what really happened, and then you clean it up.

We now have proof that the Kodak Adjustment of the summer holiday really does work. Several years earlier – when there were two children, not four, and they were much younger – they were taken out to the same Saskatchewan farm we have recently left. And when we asked this time if they remembered anything about that previous visit, all four recited a tale about a terrific ride their grandmother had given them in an old wheelbarrow. Two weren't there and two were too young to remember the actual incident, but they all remember perfectly the photograph. They are laughing in the picture. They "remember" the farm fondly.

And soon Kodak will reprocess this summer and return it to us in the form we choose to remember it. Years from now they will remember the way they laughed and played along the north shore of Lake Superior, how they giggled while bouncing in the thick salt water of Saskatchewan's Little Manitou Lake, how they screamed with delight as they literally flew down a Manitoba waterslide. They will recall fondly the little pike the boy caught in Minnesota, the beauty of the waterfalls we camped by in Wisconsin, the surprising beaches along the north side of Lake Michigan. There will be pictures of them waving, smiling, fishing, hiking, and camping.

Thanks to the Kodak Adjustment, there will be no permanent record of the fights, the tantrums, the times the vehicle with the Ontario plates pulled over to the side of the road and the driver waded back into the maw of the average family to hand out a little frontier justice. There is no photograph, mercifully, of the time the "CHECK ENGINE" light flashed red on a stretch of highway that had no gas stations at either end. Nor is there one of the lunging snake that bit a small child in Minnesota as the youngster was bending down to pick it up. In time, there being no lasting proof of these moments, they will cease entirely to exist, thanks to the Kodak Adjustment.

We will soon forget the broken tentpole, the mosquitoes, the constant slam of a camp toilet door, perhaps
even what it is like to be travelling through North
Dakota in 34°C weather without air-conditioning.

Some other things, however, we would like never to
forget, and it is unfortunate that there will be no permanent record to pull out and stare longingly at on a cold
winter's evening.

I wish, for example, I could show you the radio station in Fort Frances, Ontario, that will bump the CBC
"World at Six" in order to pass on a message to the
people of a certain Lake of the Woods island that "Crystal has an ear infection so we won't be at the dock until
8:30 tomorrow." That's having your summer priorities
straight.

And I wish now I had taken a picture of the old man
from Germany I came across sitting on a piece of drift-
wood one morning staring out over Lake Superior.

He and his wife had been on the road since he'd
retired. Last year it was eastern Europe and the Soviet
Union. This year it will be Canada, the United States,
and Mexico.

Canada wasn't his favourite country so far – that
honour goes to Greece – but Canada, in his opinion, was
"the cleanest" country in the world.

Imagine him remembering us that way already – and
he hasn't even got his pictures back yet.

For six months now, the Central Canadian has been
promising the ocean, and today is the day he must
deliver.

For six months the Central Canadian has lain down late at night in short beds and talked the innocents who refuse to sleep into giving sleep one more try on the promise that they will dream of what it will be like when we get to the ocean. They will dream of the sound it makes and the way it tastes and the magnificent creatures that live in it and the great treasures that wash up on its shores and the way children can run forever in the tickling wind and sweet light that is found there and only there, only at the ocean.

They have talked about the ocean from the moment they left Central Canada and now they are almost there. For a thousand miles the younger ones have been asking the same question: "Is that it?"

They thought the St. Lawrence was the ocean. They thought one particularly wide stretch along the Saint John River was the ocean. They thought the toll bridge leading into the city of Saint John was heading out over the ocean. And every time the Central Canadian got to say "No, that's not it – not yet," he sighed, knowing that all too soon it would indeed be it and his terrible secret would be out.

He knows less about the ocean that he does about the rings of Saturn.

This is, of course, a problem common to Central Canadians, but the one we are talking about here has more problems than most. He did not even see an ocean until the end of his sixteenth summer, when he and three high school pals took off in a green '51 Ford, heading for Cape Cod. When they got to the ocean, they were as awkward with it as they would have been with the girls who were rumoured to be there. Didn't have a clue what to make of it. They were Central Canadians, after all, and to them a large body of water was one you had to turn on your back to swim across.

They did not understand undertows. They did not understand tides. They did not recognize a single thing that washed up on the shores.

It hardly mattered back in 1964. But it most certainly does matter today. These kids who think the ocean is just around the next corner believe that the man taking them there has salt water running through his veins. He has told them about giant squid and friendly whales and ship-wrecks and bottles with mysterious messages and tidal pools filled with more magic that the window tank at the pet store in the neighbourhood shopping mall. He has sold them a bill of goods picked up from poetry and the movies and his own imagination – and today he must deliver.

We have two hours to kill before the ferry departs for Digby, and the young woman in the information booth at the Reversing Falls has suggested a short run out to Saint's Rest beach where, yes, we can taste salt water.

"We're going to the ocean," the Central Canadian announces, suitably cheered.

The road eventually becomes gravel, then dips down on to a harsh shoreline where there is sand and surf, but not a single seagull. That's not quite true, there is a seagull. The dog finds it. It has been dead for some time, and she starts to roll in it.

The kids run along the beach, but the wind whips sand in needles against their bare legs.

The only thing the Central Canadian finds washed up that he recognizes is a used condom, but he refuses to point it out.

He can't explain how tides work. He warns about the undertow, but can't say what, exactly, it is.

Disappointed, they all head back to wait for the ferry. At the ferry there is also a small beach, and people are wandering about at low tide. The Central Canadian leads the kids down, hoping to recover, but though he stares into the pools and small things move, he hasn't got a clue what they are.

"Hey!" a voice shouts from a distance. "You kids wanna see something?"

The voice belongs to a burly young man. He wears a jean jacket with the arms cut and and a tattoo. But he is not holding a sawed-off shotgun – it is a rock that, when he drops it, rings like glass. Carefully he explains to the children how the rock was formed and how it came to be here. He takes them on a tour. He shows them how to watch for sea worms. He picks a rock up and shows them the small shrimp-like creatures that whales eat. He explains how they eat them. He sees a small hole and says it contains a big clam. He digs down, inserts his finger, twists, and up pops a big clam.

Off he wanders, the children of the Central Canadian following along, mesmerized.

The Central Canadian stares from where he stands, his pants rolled up over his knees, wondering if he finally understands how an undertow works.

We found the isolated ocean campground in Maine in the same way most do – by word of mouth. Campers near Saint John told us about it and passed on their map as if we were being initiated into a secret society.

"It's the most unbelievable campground we've ever been in," they said. "The guy who runs it is named Mike. Very strict. Some strange rules, but it's well worth it."

Being the sort of people who don't need strange rules –
like maybe no noise, no kids, no fighting, no junk food,
no dogs, no fiddling with your hair for two hours – we
figured we'd take a pass and head, instead, for Bar Harbor.
But then we stopped in at Charlie's Lobster Hut ($3.95 a
pound). Charlie – an old retired fisherman with the eyes
of a newborn – thought it wild that a family of six was
travelling around in a truck with more living space than
his little shack where he and his four brothers had been
born and raised before he turned it into a roadside stop.

"Where ya goin'?" he wanted to know.

"Bar Harbor."

"You don't wanna go there. Here, I'll give you a
place."

The same directions. The same warning. "Mike's very
strict. You follow his rules or he kicks you the hell out.
It's less than five miles from here. You gotta at least go
take a look."

What's five more miles when you're already a thousand over your pre-paid rental limit? We headed off,
took a couple of lefts, and came to a dirt road with proof
that we had arrived – a huge sign: "NO RADIOS."

And no office, either. Eventually, a large, muscular
man under a drooping straw hat barged through some
pine trees, walked up, and introduced himself as Mike.

"Where's the office?" I asked.

He lifted his straw hat off his head. "Right under
here."

"What do we do?"

"Drive around 'til you find something you like. I'll
find you."

We drove around, and we liked everything: a harsh,
thundering coastline, high and rocky points, campsites

so set apart from each other they seemed like country estates compared to the squeezed fields we had come from, a view of the open sea from each one. We set up, and Mike soon bulled through the trees.

"How'd you hear about this?" he asked, the tone as close to accusing as to curious.

"Campers in New Brunswick."

Mike grunted, "I did a survey last year. More'n two-thirds get here by word of mouth."

"It's a beautiful campground."

"It's a wilderness park," Mike corrected. "No one disturbs anything here. Not the shore. And not each other. You play your radio, I throw you out."

"Mind if I ask why?"

"People don't come here to hear your music. They come to listen to the ocean. You turn your radio on, I turf you out."

I wanted to hug him. After fifteen hundred miles of New Kids on the Block and local Morning Zoo programs, he had finally cut off the speakers.

Mike kept talking – about how he'd delivered his seven children himself, about the toilets he cleans twenty times a day, about the seal pups he saw on the point – and just when the thought struck that perhaps radios are banned because Mike is himself a talk show, he took his $20, bulled back into the pines, and was gone. We were left alone to eat Charlie's lobsters by the campfire, to explore, and then to find out what one listens to when the radio's not working.

The kids ran out over the high rocks and came back with urchins, a starfish, and, they claimed, a whale sighting. I tracked down Mike and asked him if this was possible. He treated it like a dumb question. "There's everything out there. You just have to sit and watch."

Later, in the evening, we did just that. There were ducks on the water and fireflies in the long grass. It was dark but for the sweep of a single, distant lighthouse, until one of the kids pointed to a huge yellow ball bobbing in the water to the east. "Look at the sunset!"

"It's the moon," someone younger whispered.

We lay on the rocks and watched the full moon rise high in the sky. We stared up at the stars and talked about the chances of life elsewhere, certain it could never compare with life here, not at this moment.

"What's that sound?" the youngest said.

"What sound?"

He made a sound, a strange, high-pitched hum, that rose and dropped. "That," he said. "Is that what whales make?"

"Maybe," he was told. "Let's all listen."

And we did, hearing whatever we wanted – the sea at night the most amazing radio program any of us had ever heard.

I thought I had read somewhere that the Freak Sideshow was a thing of the past. No more Seal Boy, no more big, goofy-looking guys who can load a dozen golf balls into their mouths and spit them out over the crowd, no more Rubber Girl bending her fingers back to her wrist.

Thirty years ago, in a farmer's field to the west of a small town, I once paid a quarter to enter a pitch-black tent and stare helplessly into a dark pool that held the Hippo That Sweats Blood.

"We cannot reveal this strange and bizarre creature to the sunlight," the man who had taken our quarters shouted out in the dark. "If he sweats, he dies, cruelly drained of his life juices!"

You cannot see such things anymore, but that does not mean there are no more freaks to be found on the midway. And while it is one thing to see a blood-sweating hippo, it is quite another to come across your own eight-year-old daughter hanging out of a midway booth barking at the passers-by to try their luck. But that is what happened, and this – as much as one parent can piece together – is how it happened:

Little travelling midways that once set up in farmers' fields now set up in rather more accessible places like mall parking lots and schoolyards. This particular one came on a hot weekend when the grass needed cutting and put up a few rides and a small strip of games at the side of the local arena, a short enough bike ride away that an absent-minded parent – say, one lost in the sports pages – might say "Sure, go ahead, I'll catch up to you later," when the two youngest come screaming.

But *catching up later* is supposed to imply finding them laughing at the balloon animals a clown is making, not surrounded by tattoos and beer bellies and roll-your-own cigarettes and tight jeans, knife scars, chain wallets; not to come across an eight-year-old girl who slept the night before on a mound of stuffed animals and is asking now if she can slip home for a few minutes to fix her lipstick.

"C'mon! Step right up!" her little voice squeaks out over the ghetto blasters and gasoline generators and screams from the anti-gravity ride.

"She was crying 'cause she had no money," a thick man in a baseball cap and a dangling smoke says. "So I says, 'Well, hop in, honey, and earn some.'"

Her younger brother is nowhere to be found. He turns up later looking – and smelling – as if he has been rolling around in a stable, which is exactly where he has been, *working* with the man who runs the pony rides under the far maples. He has no time for treats. "I have to work," he says in an irritated voice that echoes strangely of my own, and heads back.

For a long time you stand there reminding yourself that this is a suburb of a modern city and these are strangers and the judicious thing to do is win the children through bribery and whisk them away, safely back to the suburban cocoon. But who can deny the draw of the Freak Sideshow?

For a long time, you sneak around in the beating sun pretending to watch them work but in fact watching them survive, spying on your own children until, late in the afternoon, a heavy man with a huge moustache and a snake tattoo comes over from his own booth, puts his hands on his hips, and says: "She makes a great Carney girl."

"She's only eight," you say, wondering why pride is in your voice.

"Yah," he says. "They usually don't run away with the Carneys 'til around eleven."

You turn and he is already walking away, his sides jiggling with his own little joke.

Night comes and she is handed a two-dollar bill and the boy is given a free pony ride, and off we head for home. It is a remarkable night, the air so cool on burnt skin, the moon thinning, a pastel sky that looks like it should be hanging over an African plain, not a suburban city. The boy, exhausted, rides the handlebars while you push, his free hand filled with the cotton candy that came at the end of his work day.

"How come," he asks, "when you put it in your mouth it disappears?"

You don't know, but he offers the second-last bite anyway.

And he is right. When it is in your hand, you cannot hold on for long. And just when the taste is sweetest, it vanishes forever.

Roots

The first time I saw it, I thought it was the ugliest place on earth. A northern exposure. Too damp. Too steep. Overgrown. No rocks to dive off; no sand to walk on. The waterline beginning the instant the hemlock gave up.

I had come to this ugly patch of Muskoka Highland because, back then, I would do anything to be with a certain young woman. Even if anything meant mosquitoes and raspberry-cane scratches and tromping around on slippery moss behind a man, her father, who saw a dock where I could see only deadheads, a cedar deck where I could see only poplar scrub and toadstools.

His $1,200 had been the only offer on this sloping pie-shaped government lot on Camp Lake. That should have told him something. But so determined was this quiet high-school teacher to have his own sacred spot on the water that he probably would have bid against himself to win it. For him, it was a lifelong dream come true. Here he would build his fires. Here he would work with his hands. Here he would fall asleep to the soft kiss of surfacing trout, awake to the alarm of the loon. For me, it was nothing of the sort. I was, but did not know it then, a cottage snob.

I had come from a strangely privileged background, one that had everything to do with circumstance and nothing whatsoever to do with money. I knew no one else from my baby-boom generation who had been toilet-trained on an outdoor privy and who could remember being taught how to turn a tap and flip a light switch after we moved from the bush into town. My father was a lumberman who worked in Ontario's magnificent and wild Algonquin Park. My grandfather had been chief ranger. For me, the park could not only never be replaced, it must never be challenged.

How could anything ever compare? The old ranger's reward for blazing the trail that would one day become Highway 60 through the park had been permission to select the lot of his choice on which to build the place he would live. He went to the heart of his beloved park, Lake of Two Rivers, and chose a long, high point facing south where the morning sun would walk up gently slanting rocks on the east side and the evening sun would pour its rich, thick light over high, dramatic rocks to the west.

He built a magnificent two-storey log home on the highest point of the rocks; built it and a beautiful granite-and-quartz fireplace and three outer cabins and an icehouse with his own hands and wrote the date and signed his name on the last piece of trim he set on September 10, 1940.

It seemed he had created this Eden for the dozens of grandchildren who swarmed over the point each summer, a few of whom were lucky enough to live there each year from the moment school in the town let out until it let back in. My older brother and I built a baseball diamond around the woodpiles. My sister and I built an entire miniature world on a sheltered bay by the point, with small roads and stone steps and small graveyards for minnows and tadpoles and newts and crayfish where, if you had any decency about you, you spoke low and stepped carefully.

It was a world of coal oil lamps, huge ice blocks packed in sawdust, fresh trout, Archie comics, and deer that ate from your hand. You awoke to the slam of a screen door, fell asleep to the howl of the timber wolves on the far side of the lake.

And this – this pitiful, overgrown, ugly hill on the side of a lake that couldn't be bothered forming a proper shore – *this* was supposed to compete with such a memory?

The sixties twisted into the seventies. A bulldozer rammed a rough road in to the lake that had no shore. The teacher retired, and he and his wife began to construct their outrageous dream, while I shook my head in dismay. They laid footings and hauled lumber, and, eventually, a small cottage went up. He built his deck. He dug a hole on the only space that wasn't rock and put up an outhouse. He built a crib in winter and a dock over the sunken crib in the summer. Furniture came from old relatives and from an insatiable urge to scavenge back-road dumps. Water would still be carried up from the lake, but there would be electricity.

Gradually, the hill took on a new personality, yet it could never compete with the old ranger's log cottage on Lake of Two Rivers. It did not matter that the real cottage was no longer there (the ranger had died, an American had bought the place, and, eventually, it was torn down in a fit of returning the park to its original state), for the footings and chinking and cribs of Lake of Two Rivers were still solid and lasting in my mind.

A hundred Teen Town dances later and the young woman and I were no longer teenagers but married. Too soon, it seemed, we had four children. Much too soon, the retired teacher died, and, naturally, we were expected to step in and help his wife become to the cottage what he had been: keeper, handyman, curator, lover. The real question, of course, was whether or not this pitiful little attempt at a cottage could ever step in and become to me what the old ranger's cottage had been. A selfish thought, but I did not know then that a cottage is a state of mind, not a fixed address. The cottage is an idea that snuggles up against the soul of Canadians the way Brighton does to Britons and possum-hunting does to Alabamans. It is who we are, our statement on the bush and the north and the seasons. It is the way we homestead on summer, as if it might be somehow possible to build a better life away from the April muck and November sleet and January hopelessness. It is the way we shake off our cluttered city lives and are permitted to pioneer momentarily away from the madness and stress. It is where we would live, if only we could figure out how.

It matters not whether it's called a cottage or a camp, whether owned or rented or, best of all, borrowed; it matters not whether we speak of $700,000 solar-heated three-car-garage glass inventions on the shores of Georgian Bay or a tent struck on the shores of the Qu'Appelle River. A true cottage finds you, not the other way around.

And that's just what happened with this rustic little cottage on the sloping side of the lake with no shore. Slowly the place crept up on me. It took years, but that, I suppose, is the great curiosity of rituals that matter: when they first come along, we fail to recognize them for what they are. But then, one day, after a decade or more of working up to it, you find yourself breathing deeply when the door bursts open on a cold and musty cottage. Someone always says the bugs are either better or worse than last year. They are never the same. You walk to the raspberry patches and lay grand plans for pies, knowing that, in fact, no raspberry will ever make it out in any container other than a child's stomach. The kids check in the bay for the sunken boat that has been there for twenty years. They look under the dock for the snapping turtle that collects a thousand missed heartbeats a year.

I tried to explain to these children why my cottage was so much more special. I would tell them how the old ranger they never knew would stand at the dock and watch us swim on our own the distance between the boardwalk and booms, and how it was worth a dollar to anyone who could. If you could swim this distance, the reward was also to swim beyond the boom, and if you could swim from the boom to a distant rock, you were qualified then to begin diving off the high rocks to the west.

My own children demanded a dollar when they, too, could swim between the pier dock their grandfather had built and the small floating dock their mother had built, then two dollars if they could swim from there to the diving platform of the next cottage down. This done, they decided it qualified them to try to swim across the bay. It was only when I realized that some of them might someday be measuring their own children in such a manner – telling them, God forbid, about an old eccentric they never knew – that I realized it is not the place but the experience we hand down.

Their grandparents' tiny cottage on the side of a hill – northern exposure, no shoreline – has been twisting as deep into their own souls as the old ranger's place had in mine. And if it is the experience that is important, not the place, then it suddenly no longer mattered so much that someone had come and bought the ranger's place away from us and torn it down, taken it away and burned what was left. The experience no one could touch, not with bulldozers, not with fire, certainly not with money.

I had to learn to see this other place through the eyes of my own children. Long into summer nights, I have stood along this harsh shoreline with each of them, three girls and a boy, as each child passed through that remarkable phase that comes only to five-year-olds, when they stand, shaking and shivering, one bare foot scratching the bites on the other calf, their hands around a fishing rod while bats swoop out of the high spruce. Sometimes we hear radios playing all the way from the far island. Sometimes we hear the trout rolling as they feed. Sometimes it seems as if the stars hang from the trees and are thicker than the mosquitoes. Sometimes a child even catches something.

The Canadian summer is a transitory joy, one so fleeting that even its difficulties are treasured. It is our secret time, the two or three or, with luck, four weeks when we believe we are our truest selves. It is our sweetest thought, one held in parentheses by the opening up and the closing up, the season beginning with sparklers and ending in embers, when suddenly, without warning, the seasons reverse on you. The leaves no longer shade but reveal; relief now is to be found inside rather than out, in fire rather than water. On an October morning so cold that the black lake steams, an outdoor toilet loses entirely its July charm.

This is when we take summer down to the small shed and put it away with a half-tank of mixed gasoline, a single flipper, and three reels that somebody with half a brain should be able to fix. This is when the air comes out of the cottage, when you pull the small plastic plugs with your teeth and stand stomping inner tubes and plastic boats while your own stale breath from early July hisses back at you.

It has only been in the last year that I have come to understand that the cottage – any cottage – is where children who are lucky enough to get to one keep their summers. If summers are the jewels of their little lives, then the cottage is the velvet box where summer is stored.

This I learned in the dead of summer, at the end of one of those heavy, hot weeks when the days seem to follow each other with the loyalty and rhythm of parading elephants. My oldest daughter was sitting down by the water in what has, over the years, been reconstructed into her own private cottage-within-the-cottage.

There she had hauled in sand to make a beach that mostly washed away. She had strung a rope from a branch for swinging out over the water and letting go with a scream. She had built a dock that wobbled. She had put in her own benches and, using spruce boughs, built her own beach umbrella for shade. The branches had turned brown as rust and the needles were falling off, but she sat below it with a comic on her lap staring out over the water.

"Don't ever sell this place," she said. "I want my children to come here." ·

Sell it? We don't even own it. But none of this would mean anything to her. The place owns her.

That lesson repeated itself over Christmas. We were home in Ottawa, typical plugged-in suburbanites on a cold December evening, and the power went off. One moment all was completely normal – television roaring, ghetto blasters pounding, Christmas lights blinking – and the next moment it was not normal at all. It was totally black, completely silent. No one said a word until a match could be located and struck, producing a nearly forgotten light, pale and yellow, that sent shadows leaping against the kitchen wall.

"Neat!" someone said.

A flashlight was found, and with the flashlight two ornamental coal oil lamps were brought from another room and lighted. The suburban kitchen filled with a liquid yellow colour it had never before known. The children stared at each other and their surroundings as if they were suddenly guests in a magic house.

"It's like being at the cottage," one of them noticed.

It was not just the light, but the silence – as if for once in this bedroom-community two-storey, you might hear a squirrel scamper across the roof rather than the burst of a laugh track from the television room. The two youngest children ran with the flashlight for their comforters, brought them down, wrapped themselves up with exaggerated squirms of delight and asked for a fire.

While the fire stuttered and snapped, they filled the space usually taken by television and cassette tapes by talking about their most treasured moment of the year just past.

"Remember the snapping turtle?" someone said.

"Remember the deer tracks by the sand pit?" someone answered.

I went and stood by the window, remembering another house in the bush when these same lamps would cast just enough light for an old ranger to work on his crossword puzzles and an old woman to prepare her Christmas baking. My mother would be testing the wood stove oven with the back of her hand. My father would be due soon from the mill. A brother would be reading comic books; a sister would have a jigsaw puzzle out that had been put together and taken apart so often, certain pieces looked like splayed books.

Once, as adults, my sister and I had gone back in search of our special place by the point. It was stunningly overgrown, and though we did find one spot where it looked as if stone steps had once been laid out, it was now like a Mayan ruin. The point could not live up to the memory, but the memory had not been harmed in the least by this realization. If anything, it was all the more valuable because now, it was all we would ever have of those times.

These children in their comforters by the fire were talking, I realized, of the most beautiful place I now know on earth. It is their perfect childhood memory still being formed.

"Remember the big toad?" a small voice wondered.

But before anyone could, the power surged back on. Lights, television, tapes, buzzers, clocks . . .

"Boooooo!" the children shouted.

It was a false alarm. The power failed; the coal oil lamps regained their place; the children cheered. And while they returned to their cottage memories, their mother and I quietly left the room to the crackling fire and their low, excited voices. And we walked about the suburban house turning off every electrical switch we could find.

Acknowledgments

The author gratefully acknowledges the generosity of *The Ottawa Citizen* in granting permission to reprint certain columns. Gratitude is also expressed to *Canadian Living* for permission to reprint material which originally appeared in that magazine. Thanks to Margaret Mills, Linda LeGroulx, Jean Sprott, Barbara Dalton, Jane Fox, Ellen MacGregor, and dozens of anonymous teachers and social workers for their wonderul suggestions. Thanks to Lucinda Vardey for advice and encouragement, Douglas Gibson for enthusiasm, and Sarah Reid for caring so much about the words. But above all, thanks to the *Citizen* and particular editors – Nelson Skuce, Scott Honeyman, Graham Parley, Murdoch Davis, David Evans, Gordon Fisher, Peter Calamai – for letting me roam at large and asking for more when the column stumbled, by accident, into the bizarre world of power parenting.